Fishing in America

FISHING

by Charles F. Waterman | A Ridge Press Book

in AMERICA

Holt, Rinehart and Winston | New York

Editor-in-Chief: Jerry Mason
Editorial Director: Adolph Suehsdorf
Art Director: Albert Squillace
Managing Editor: Moira Duggan
Art Associate: David Namias
Art Production: Doris Mullane
Picture Editor: Marion Geisinger

Technical Adviser: Mary Shepard

Published in the United States of America in 1975 by Holt, Rinehart and
Winston, Publishers, 383 Madison Avenue, New York, New York 10017, U.S.A.
Published simultaneously in Canada by Holt, Rinehart and Winston of Canada, Limited.
Waterman, Charles F
    Fishing in America.
    "A Ridge Press book."
    Bibliography: p.
    Includes index.
    1. Fishing—North America—History. I. Title.
SH462.W3   799.1'097   75-5473
ISBN 0-03-014186-9
Printed and bound in Italy by Mondadori Editore, Verona.

To my wife Debie,
who feels all fishing research
should be done firsthand.

Contents

Foreword

Angling has been only a footnote to history,
building its own traditions in the shadows of more momentous
activities. There have been chroniclers through the
centuries, yet most of them were intrigued only by small aspects of
the sport, so that we have patches
of meticulous detail and great fields of mystery.

It is likely that the greatest anglers have been unknown, for
the most complex fishing endeavors are often
private sport—and, indeed, there was a long period when fishing for
amusement was considered a trifling pastime
of no credit to its followers. The only remembered fishermen
of angling's beginnings are those
who recorded their progress in print, and their teachers for
the most part have been nameless.

There have been so many kinds of angling,
beginning in so many different places, that the masters of
another era may never have heard of each other,

even as the brown-trout scholar of today cannot name the masters
of black-bass fishing. And since
all sport angling is dependent on self-imposed restrictions,
achievement in one direction may be of little
interest to an expert who seeks his own challenges in another.

The tackle of bygone years has
only recently been of sufficient interest to attract collectors,
and many of the true treasures are
still unrecognized. The angling historian can still work in a
field of new discoveries, and soon
learns he can only scratch the surface in a lifetime.

This account of America's fishing
has gained much from the research of Mary Shepard and her
husband Warren, both of whom are immersed
in the meticulous detail of the development of rods and reels; their
tracing of the angler's progress in America is
well illustrated by their superb collection of antique tackle.

—Charles F. Waterman

1. Primitive Fish

and Men

The gar lay in close order, more than one hundred of them, their flattened snouts facing upstream in the sluggish dark water. They were so nearly motionless that they might have been waterlogged sticks of wood, some suspended near the surface and others a little deeper. They were spaced with mathematical precision, none of them feeding, their fin movements almost imperceptible. All were nearly the same size, about two feet long, and the sun brought no reflection from their ancient armor.

Upstream a few yards the flow was more pronounced, the slow current bearing a few bubbles as it was pinched between vertical reeds growing so thickly that they formed nearly solid walls. There was a gap in the growth a little downstream from the flotilla of prehistoric fish, and in the ragged opening were three dark, motionless lumps, easily mistaken for floating debris, but actually the nostrils and eye knobs of a great reptile in silent ambush, its length extending far back into the reeds.

Where the creek narrowed above the gar, a grotesque stilt-legged bird stood on a few fallen reeds broken by earlier flood waters, its dagger beak shaped like that of the featherless flying reptiles that soared on leathery wings in prehistoric times. The bird watched for primitive minnows that schooled, scattered, and regrouped again in current that curled into the deeper pool where the gar held.

But the age of man had come and the great bird wore feathers. The gar had changed little in millions of years and the great reptile at the pool's edge had outlived even larger reptiles that had not adapted to Earth's tortured changes.

Most of the ancient residents rested in the great swamp, but the human newcomer intruded stealthily. He appeared at first only as a black bump above the dark green of the pool's border and he saw the raft of gar through the reed tips that moved slightly in the breeze. His face was broad and the color of mahogany and his straight black hair touched his naked shoulders. He moved a little sidewise in a soundless glide, his bare feet feeling instinctively for solid purchase in the drowned bases of the shoulder-high reeds.

When the nearest of the garfish was in easy range, he moved the spear point forward, the haft shoulder height, then cocked his arm smoothly and fired the spear in a controlled sweep, holding to the line with one hand.

The spear chugged into the water and into a gar. The other fish scattered and went deeper. The reptile simply sank, leaving three tiny surface circles for an instant. The bird squawked and irritably flapped off, barely above the swamp growth, and the man retrieved his kill. The surface commotion brought quick attention from the bottom. An ancient fish, its weaving dorsal almost the full length of its body and its needle teeth showing in an anticipatory grin, rose under the threshing gar, but when the spear drew it out of sight the big bowfin sank again to settle flat against the muddy bottom. Like the gar, the bowfin had changed but little through the centuries, a remnant from ages long before man.

The man backed away to solid ground. He smelled of wood smoke and a little of smoked garfish. He turned toward his camp and glanced at the summer sky. Across the immensity of boiling thunderheads was a single straight contrail, the wake of a jet airplane bound for Colombia from Miami. The young Seminole wore trunks from a department store and his gig's head was twentieth-century steel, but his skills had

*Opening pages: Primitive rivers flowed
through virgin forests, descended from mountain
snows, were fed by bogs and valley creeks.
They spread into wide valleys and prairies to
reach distant seas, nurturing fish that
ranged from the cold-water trout of high places to
sluggish bottom dwellers of lowland
marshes. Unchanged by early man, waters waited
for civilization's dams and drainage.*

persisted unchanged for thousands of years.

The earliest evidence of primitive man shows that he was a fisherman; most cultures at one period or another seem to have been dependent on a fish supply. Fishing methods, once established, changed slowly. Even as newer tools appeared among archaeological traces of man's development, it seems clear that he retained his old fishing techniques. Indians and Eskimos still apply today some of the methods they used at about the time their ancestors arrived on the North American continent, although, of course, they now employ some modern materials in constructing their equipment. In some situations advanced tools are unnecessary, or even inferior to what went before, and when laws finally were needed to protect land game from new hunting devices that were too deadly, other laws were introduced to protect fish from the ancient methods of early humans. The hook, spear, and net were so efficient that they threatened to reduce a fish supply already decimated by devastating changes in the environment.

When fishing became sport instead of labor, the most modern equipment was partly a self-imposed handicap. And although it might be designed for greater efficiency, that efficiency was applied only within a strict set of rules. Fish are simple creatures, and despite anglers' romantic assessments of their intelligence their capture involves elementary processes. The development of angling techniques is chiefly a refinement of old practices. There has been no revolutionary fishing innovation to compare with the invention of gunpowder as it affected hunting.

The very first living things are obscured in the mists of millions of years past, but they must have begun in the warm seas that once covered much of the earth.

The first fossilized creatures appeared in the rocks of the Cambrian era five hundred million years ago—although life had existed much longer before then than it has endured since. From the Cambrian period, through the Ordovician, to the end of the Silurian, one hundred and seventy-five million years later, life was in the warm oceans and not on the land. Then with the Cambrian period came plates, skins, and protective shells and since then the archaeological record has been continuous.

It was in the Silurian period that the mountain ranges rose and oceans became confined, fed by rain-water streams. Probably the first true vertebrate fishes had their beginning in fresh water; among the most primitive of living ones are the lancelets, lampreys, and hag fishes, which do not have true jaws.

As the oceans receded into their confining basins they left sediments that welcomed the migration of plant life from sea to land. The movement was slow, but the suspended plants of the sea found footing, and during the Devonian period, beginning three hundred and twenty-five million years ago, the sea plants evolved into ferns and trees to form the shores of fresh-water lakes and streams, eventually to help bind them and to slow the movement of water.

The precarious life in rain-fed creeks encouraged fish adapted to drought. The lungfishes breathed in hibernation on dried and cracked bottoms, and other fish used leg-like fins to walk to remaining pools. A survivor of such creatures is the "walking" catfish, really a fish that squirms and wriggles with directional purpose. It is a menace to other species and halted only by low temperatures.

Some of those early fishes survived in only slightly altered form, and the evolution of others has moved in so many directions that it is difficult to say which is more advanced than the other. If survival is taken as the primary measure of an organism's quality, some of our most primitive fishes are outstanding examples of design. For the past twenty-five thousand years there has been no marked evolutionary change in the native fishes of North America. The first known men of the continent sought most of the species existing today. If there is an "Age of Fishes," it may still be going on, for there are forty thousand kinds today, and they are most numerous of the vertebrates. They range from the whale shark, the largest of which have been estimated at one hundred and fifty thousand pounds, to a Philippine lake fish less than half an inch long. America's mosquito fish is only three-fourths of an inch long at maturity.

The lack of bony skeletons in many ancient aquatic creatures meant that they left a scant fossil record in stone. The more elemental of today's fishes—the sharks, rays, skates, and chimaeras—have skeletons of cartilege. Others, such as the sturgeon and the bowfin, have become partly bony. Fish with perfect bones, the Teleostei, are most important to the modern fisherman, for nearly all game fish are so classified.

Today's gar, whose armor-like scales are tough enough to have been used by early American farmers to cover their wooden plowshares, looks like an artist's conception of a prehistoric fish, although among recognized game fish the tarpon has the closest actual link to the past. This is the fourteen-foot Portheus, a relative of the herrings which lived among the enormous reptiles of another age, yet looked astonishingly like the modern fish. With a slight reloca-tion of the pelvic fin and the addition of a dorsal fin, Portheus could almost pass for the Silver King.

Evolution took varied turns during the eons in which the waters flooded and ebbed. Amphibians took to the land as fleshy fins became feet and legs, but they retained their rapport with water.

Since reptiles also developed from fish-like creatures it is impossible to say whether the highly specialized tuna, for instance, is more advanced than the alligator. The most revered of game fishes often are less resourceful than scorned bottom grubbers and may be lower on the scale of intelligence as man measures it. On the other hand, because water supports more firmly than air, large sea creatures have survived in simpler forms than terrestrial species, and as a result the angler often is involved with heavier game than the hunter on land.

Although higher forms appear to have evolved from fishes, the routes of development were broken by changes in world conditions. For reasons not now clear there were many cases of land animals that turned back to the water and regained the long-gone characteristics of distant ancestors.

Great mammals such as the whales, porpoises, and seals have exchanged legs for fins and spend part or all of their lives at sea. Otters and beavers have the characteristics of land dwellers, with the addition of specialized tails which serve the same purposes as caudal fins, and may be changing either toward dry-land or full-time water residence.

The fresh-water origin of some fishes may be preserved in anadromous species that spend much of their lives in salt water but must reproduce in fresh. The Atlantic salmon may be reverting from salt to fresh water, for it must spawn in fresh-

*Garfish with armor-like scales
lives today as representative of primitive fish,
able to stay in waters too warm or
polluted for more respected modern species.
Spoonbill (below left) feeds upon small
water life and retains skeletal structure of ancient
ancestors. Tadpoles are believed to
display evolution in capsule form and demonstrate
life's dependence upon water.*

*American Indians displayed
some of their cleverest devices in fishing. Traps
and nets were made from branches, and
spears were developed especially
for pursuit of water creatures. Canoes
sometimes carried fire for spearing at night.
Some cultures were almost completely
dependent upon fishing, and history has been
read in the remains of fishing gear.*

water streams. The landlocked salmon is virtually the same fish, living proof that salt water is not essential, although it is true that seagoing fish grow much larger. Nearly all of the trouts have strains that go to sea and spawn in fresh water, although the landlocked members of their clans appear to be identical. Evolution in isolation has been responsible for the differences between Atlantic and Pacific salmons.

Although coloration, now recognized as a superficial feature, deceived early observers, the steelhead of the Pacific Coast is very closely related to the Atlantic salmon. The steelhead, simply an anadromous rainbow trout, may have been separated from the Atlantic salmon at some time when waters to the north of Canada and Alaska became so chilled that steelhead no longer used them.

Early American fishermen may have used spears to kill great fish now extinct, and their spear points have no label describing their use. But there were easier catches of smaller fish. The old campsites were near water and the fish must have been there. Men may have borrowed fish-gathering techniques from the wading birds of their time.

In a dry period, small watercourses are slowed to trickles and then become isolated ponds and pools, crowded with the fish. Where the bottom is muddy or silted, conditions are right for man's harvest.

For drying creeks those first American fishermen needed no fishing equipment. They waded into the pools, stirring up mud until the water was opaque and silt clogged the gills of imprisoned fish. Within a few minutes there were swirls on the surface as the quarry sought relief, and finally helpless fish would belly up and be tossed ashore. Species

such as the catfish would gulp at the surface and might be captured by hand or shoveled out with a flat wooden tool. In more advanced harvests the water was poisoned with crushed soapweed, buckeye, or other plants. In most cases the effect was temporary.

Where the streams were small but still running, small dams held water long enough for the roiled mud to do its work, and where water had disappeared completely there must have been fish like the bullhead that lived dormant in drying mud and were easily dug out by hand. In a much later time pioneers used the same system, and even later, farm boys waded happily in a harvest that provided a change from salt pork at the table.

Many of the fish that fed early man were windfalls for watchers patrolling the shores of sea or river. Nature occasionally forms seashore traps when a run-out tide leaves small pools that isolate and capture a school of fish that has raided the coastline and failed to find the route back to deep water. Bluefish are sometimes stranded thus, and with a little digging at low tide to remove the last of the water, the fish may be picked up alive. Or they may die in crowded exposure to a hot sun in tiny ponds.

It may be that early man robbed the osprey or its ancestors, and when waves of anadromous fish clotted the spawning rivers they could have been caught without tools or nets. West Coast Indians keyed their culture to the salmon runs. When streams are small, a man can imitate the black and grizzly bears, which fish in a series of ambushes and splashing charges. Weakened salmon nearing the end of their spawning journey can be scooped to shore by a patient man, and there is no reason to believe the primitive fisher was averse to the spawned-out dead fish that lit-

*Eskimo ice fisherman uses decoys
and lures. His survival depends almost entirely
on what the sea provides. Arctic
fishing often is done far from land and on
treacherous footing. Bone and flint
fishhooks (above left) were sometimes as
efficient as white man's steel. Ceremonial carvings
appear on Alaskan halibut hook and
float, and totem pole (left) shows captive fish.*

Night fishing from birch-bark canoes.
Indians held torches high to silhouette fish
against bottom for spearing. Lights
attracted small fish that brought larger quarry
within range. Spears advanced from
simple fire-hardened sticks to precise instruments
with barbed points. Bow and arrow (with
retrieving line attached), atlatl or throwing stick, and
three-pronged leister were other fishing tools.

tered the shores, sometimes in windrows.

From the little mud and stone dams it was but a step to those of brush and logs, and once the dam was made to turn or hold the fish it was but a step to crude traps of brush, stones, and stakes. From the artificial dam it was only a step to a woven net of reeds, grasses, vines, small branches, or inner bark; and the vine was a ready-made line for the day when man learned to use bait. It was a long while before he had hooks, but a bait sometimes worked without them.

Most early fish traps evidently were of the wing type, with fences in shallow water angling to a small opening through which fish could be driven or enticed into a small pen for spearing or catching by hand. The first Europeans in America found Indians using such structures. These traps left no sign for modern study, since their materials rot. Some Indian traps were miniatures for small fish, complete with removable funnel entrances, so that the fish inside could be reached easily. There were simple, bag-shaped traps made of branches which were towed by canoes. In Pennsylvania, boughs were lashed together and dragged toward the mouths of traps to force fish into them. Some Indians had "live pens" where fish were stored against future need.

In their headlong upstream race with death, the Pacific salmon were especially vulnerable to simple barricades or weirs, structures which would hold them to be caught or speared by a variety of methods. Alaskan Indians began such a weir by felling a large tree across a stream, and then setting stakes against it from the upstream side, one end firmly imbedded against the bottom, the other end projecting above the log, which was braced against the current. Fish coming upstream could not

scale the device and eventually were worn out trying. Some killed themselves in the attack. Although some salmon arrived early enough to drop back downstream for a time, the relentless spawning urge finally drove them against the wall.

"Hand fishing" required no tools or tackle, and its origins are unrecorded, but there were refinements that went far beyond the simple seizure of fish trapped in drying watercourses or pinned against barricades. Even the sleek trouts were vulnerable to the patient wader's careful hand. In England, early fishing accounts say, trout were "tickled" and then tossed ashore. It was believed they were mesmerized by the gentle stroking.

But the American system must have been more adapted to sluggish bottom victims, such as catfish, and was most practical in quiet murky waters. The fisherman waded slowly along fallen logs or undercuts, feeling gently with hands and feet. When he felt a fish he fingered it carefully until he found a satisfactory hold. In the twentieth century this method was still in use in the Midwest and South, where "noodlers" or "ticklers" found large catfish in hollow logs or underwater caves. Sometimes ropes were deftly attached to large fish imprisoned in their own resting places.

It may be that the gentle fingers of an expert actually hypnotize the victim and it may be that a fish in muddy water accepts the intrusion as that of another fish, but the required patience was a quality of hungry primitive man.

Bait could have been used before any sort of hook or gorge as a means of drawing fish into a trap or within range of a spear. Students of the earliest hunters suggest that hook-and-line angling could have been used on birds and animals before it was

employed in fishing. Large hooks of buffalo bones were reportedly used for alligators by Gulf Coast Indians in the seventeenth century. A suitable bait attached to some sort of line could be swallowed by the victim while the hunter lay in wait. If vines or grasses were the first lines, it is possible that the first fish captured by line simply swallowed large baits and were hauled out before they could disgorge the food.

But this is conjecture, because lines were highly perishable and none survives as evidence. The fishhook began as a gorge, a tool found frequently among Indian artifacts, and one of the first contrivances of ancient man. Gorges were made of bone, stone, antler, and shell, or even of wood. They are still used for some fishing, even where more modern devices are available. The simplest gorge is a straight bar, possibly with a groove near the middle where the line is attached. It is inserted lengthwise in a bait and when the bait is swallowed and the line drawn tight, it is pulled crosswise to lodge in the fish's gullet. Most of the early gorges are slightly tapered or pointed at the ends, partly to make it easier to insert them in the bait, partly to give them a better hold on the fish.

There is a similar device sometimes used in modern fishing, with the line attached well toward one end of a sharp-pointed needle-gorge. Once the bait has been taken in by the fish, a pull on the line will cause the gorge to follow the pull at a slant and, in effect, the sharp end pierces like a hook. It is held in position by the longer section, which presses against the fish's gullet on the opposite side. Such a "needle" has been used in European eel fishing.

That the modern hook developed from the gorge has been accepted by European scholars,

Fish being preserved on drying racks.

their theory being that the straight or nearly straight crosspiece was increasingly bent, and used with well-sharpened ends, until it was in effect a double hook. American progress is not so readily charted.

Ancient spear and arrow points confuse students of fishing history, because it is impossible to tell whether they were used for fish or game, although it is likely they were used for both. It has been suggested that the first fishing poles were the spears of primitive man, but there is no proof of this, either.

There is some doubt about the larger stone hooks found at ancient campsites, since they may have been used for purposes other than fishing. Shell hooks, such as those found in California, undoubtedly were for fishing and have been recovered in all stages of construction. The workman began with a rounded piece of shell, made a hole near the center, and then shaped the hook about it. Most such hooks are curved as part of a circle, and instead of an eye for the line there is a notch or groove in the shank. Crude as the tool may be, it was well designed and effective. The line groove is generally placed to give a straight pull of the point against the fish—a principle widely advertised in some modern bait hooks. Some of the shell hooks were formed into a nearly complete circle and evidently were intended as bait holders and gorges, since the points were unlikely to pierce a biting fish. Shell hooks do not appear except at the older archaeological sites.

Some of the more efficient ancient hooks were composites employing parts of wood, antler, bone, ivory, bird and animal claws, flint, or shell. The sharpened point was attached to a shank of some easily worked material.

Most were undecorated but the halibut hooks of the Northwest were often ornate works of art with ceremonial significance. They were mostly of wood and designed in V shape. In use, the V was usually suspended with one side parallel to the bottom. The barb, made of a variety of sharpened materials, was set in the lower arm, pointing upward, and the line was attached to the upper arm. Bait was fastened only to the lower section and the fish took only that part into its mouth. The section to which the line was attached was decoratively carved, usually with a mythological figure. The hooks were so buoyant that heavy sinkers were required. They were often fished in pairs with wooden spreader bars.

The first spears probably were simple sharpened sticks, then sticks whose points were hardened in fire. Barbed arrows and spears came much later. The atlatl, or throwing stick, may have been used for fishing as well as hunting; the bow certainly was used, finally with a line for retrieving the kill.

The leister is a three-pronged spear constructed so that the center point can pierce a fish deeply while the others act as a clamp, with inside barbs to prevent slippage. This form is especially effective in spearing from above, and in case of a very large target all three points can be thrust deeply. Leisters were used by both Indians and Eskimos.

The Eskimos, master mechanics with minimal materials, constructed deadly harpoons with detachable heads for whales and seals, and their toggle point was shaped to drive deeper as pull was exerted on the attached line. Such equipment worked equally well on large fish. Inflated bladders tired fish or game caught on harpoon heads, and baited hooks were suspended from floating bladders. When the fish tired from towing the float it was easily hauled into a kayak.

The Eskimo, living in an Arctic

world by choice, while other primitive American fishermen and hunters sought milder latitudes, used some of America's first artificial lures, combining an ivory or bone fish decoy with his spearmanship. The decoy, dangled through an ice hole, attracted inquisitive quarry within spear range and was a part of the "dark hut" system used by both Indians and Eskimos. The fisherman constructed a small hut of skins or reeds over his ice hole, or across a very small stream, so that downward visibility would be better, and sometimes he scattered light-colored pebbles over a dark bottom to silhouette fish. Ice holes were sometimes baited, and Eskimos blew air into them, a bubbling disturbance which evidently attracted fish.

Migratory chars, trout, and salmon of the Arctic were speared during their upstream spawning trips, and the Eskimos often waded for them in icy backwaters, their lower bodies protected by sealskin pants. Both men and women participated, and for a moment the grim gathering of food turned to boisterous sport as entire villages of splashing fishermen speared confused and milling fish.

But it was in lonely vigils where ice, sky, and water merged in a featureless pall that the Eskimo suffered for his food. He became a stoic or he failed, and although modern observers tend to cast Eskimos in a single mold of stoicism there were cases of "kayak sickness," when lonely boatmen's minds cracked during hours of motionless waiting. Men in other circumstances would call it nervous breakdown. Victims susceptible to these tensions could no longer be great hunters and fishermen, and were put to lesser tasks.

Among Indians, some of the most productive spearing was done from canoes by torchlight. The fish were strongly outlined, especially against light and shallow bottoms, and some species were actually attracted by the light.

The development of nets is hard to trace, again because most of the materials were highly perishable. Stone net weights shaped for the purpose were in use when Europeans came to America. A long line of them was found imbedded in a mud flat of the Susquehanna River, evenly spaced as evidently they had been left with a long-abandoned net. At many Indian campsites rectangular stones, smoothed from long use as patterns for net meshes, have been found. Wooden rectangles for the same purpose did not survive so well. White men found eastern Indians using some of the same knots as those of Europeans.

Gill nets were suspended near the bottom with stone sinkers and wooden floats, the latter sometimes artistically carved. Seining was often accomplished by securing one end of a net to shore and swinging the other end about with a canoe or kayak. Ice was no obstacle to the Eskimo netter. He cut holes about ten feet apart along the route the net was to be placed, and then used a pole made of baleen and inner tree-bark fibers from one opening to the next. Since the surface ice expanded downward as it became thicker, it was necessary to rig braces that held the mesh below the ice and prevented freezing. Observers have reported Eskimos removing fish from the nets with bare hands when the temperature was far below zero. The chief catches from ice sets were salmon, trout, and tom cod.

Long poles were used to swing some nets from shore. The "herring rake" was simply a long rod with spikes close set for part of its length. It was generally used from a canoe and could be swung rapidly to impale schooling fish.

Catching Salmon   Columbia River

Methods were refined through the ages, but in some locations they regressed, possibly because a fishing culture was replaced by hunters or farmers. The shell fishhooks found in California appear to have been abandoned for other tools in later years, and archaeologists find that a highly advanced fishing culture, which developed south of the Great Lakes, faded through the centuries. Along the East Coast there were tribes that must have subsisted primarily on fishing, for the bones of land animals are insignificant compared to the quantity of fish remains found at campsites. Some bone and claw hooks are considered superior to the first metal ones brought by Europeans.

The Haida and other Northwest tribes often used lines with multiple hooks—sometimes as many as a hundred. Theirs was the most advanced hook-and-line fishing in what is now the United States, and some hook design was highly advanced. The ornate halibut hook of the Northwest is nearly matched by those of some Pacific islands, a tantalizing hint of early migrations. Some historians believe the leister and harpoon were invented somewhere in the Old World and brought to America by migrants.

Indian and Eskimo beliefs in the supernatural were sometimes expressed in fables related to fish. The Pacific salmon and its migrations were understood by few if any primitive men, the mysteries being enhanced by the salmon's death after spawning. It was believed that the "salmon people" were immortal, that they dressed in salmon flesh to sacrifice themselves, and then returned to permanent residences beneath the sea where they appeared and behaved again as human beings. So the Indians who ate salmon were careful to return the skeletons unharmed to the waters, lest the salmon people be angered and refuse to run a given stream. If the bones of a salmon were destroyed, it

Salmon were the principal food resource of Indians of Columbia River, who keyed their year to the migrations. Harpoon and spear points varied with fish being sought. Traps were constructed of branches and some were towed from canoes, like trawl nets. Skillful Indians also caught fish by silting waters of a pool to clog quarry's gills, and even by hand.

could mean that a salmon person might be crippled.

Although many tribes confined their worship to land animals, some Indians who relied strongly on fish for their livelihood gave them ceremonial importance. The first fish of a seasonal run on an important salmon stream received formal recognition. It was addressed as a high-ranking visitor and eaten with ceremony. With some tribes the ceremony became so complex that a special priest was in charge. The First Salmon ceremony was best known, but there were rituals for other fishes, too.

Some northwestern Indians attributed the origin of the all-important salmon to Fog Woman, the wife of Raven, a hero often featured on totem poles. Raven and his canoe, the story goes, were lost in a thick fog when Fog Woman appeared, removed Raven's spruce-root hat from his head and caused all of the fog to disappear into it so that the sun shone and

Raven reached shore. Then Fog Woman and Raven were married, and Fog Woman created the first salmon in an inland spring.

Some tribes, such as the Haida and Tlingit, used ornately carved clubs for killing hooked halibut and harpooned seal. Other tribes used plain clubs for the purpose, and for them ceremony had little part in the practical necessity of dispatching a potentially dangerous creature from a small craft that was easily overturned. However, some Eskimos had another purpose in dispatching fish quickly, believing that the captive, if left alive, would speak ill of the fisherman.

Much fishing required boats and seamanship. In the East the birchbark canoe was an easily portaged craft that made highways of small rivers, and in larger sizes it could negotiate the open sea. On the West Coast and in the Gulf of Mexico, the dugout canoe, less portable but more durable, served

Leaping salmon (above) were speared
from long-established stands by Pacific Indians.
Modern Indian at right uses long-handled
net to fish for silver salmon on swift Klickitat River.
Platforms are lowered from cliffs and
are now held by cables instead of vines and rawhide.
Netting platforms no longer appear on
early sites along Columbia as modern power dams have
destroyed the ancient pools and rapids.

in many sizes, some of them carrying twenty persons or more. Hundreds of years later, Indians were driving dugouts with outboard motors. Most of the early models were hollowed by fire. After a section of timber had been thoroughly charred it was chopped out with simple tools. Some of the western dugouts carried high and ornamental bows.

White men could make no improvement on the design of the Indian's birchbark canoe and copied it, sometimes clumsily, for their own use. Whites also adopted the dugout for closely confined waters, and some of them were retained as pirogues along the Gulf Coast through the twentieth century. The narrow boat trails of the Mississippi delta are perfect for the pirogue and it remains a favorite of the Cajun fisherman and hunter.

Eskimos made their kayaks of skins stretched over rigid frames of wood or bone, and for light loads they are efficient craft. The Eskimo wears his kayak and is capable of righting it if it overturns without leaving his seat. His spear, harpoon, or ice hook fits in a bracket; his cockpit fits so snugly it can be made watertight, and the boatman in sealskin pants and parka can withstand terrible exposure. (Eskimos made raincoats from seal intestines before white men had slickers.) The umiak, open and much larger than the kayak, is capable of tremendous loads and was eventually used with outboard motors.

The "bullboat," a circular buffalo-skin craft constructed over a framework of bowed saplings, was a clumsy conveyance for some Indians and was an inefficient fishing boat, but its similarity to old British types caused some historians to believe there had been Welsh visitors to the continent in pre-Columbian times. There were also some tule reed boats, used mainly by lake Indians of Nevada and California.

The ravine is a narrow plunge of white water imprisoned between vertical cliffs. The torrent slopes steeply and visibly, cascades of water hurled at an angle where especially large boulders break its course. From high above on the cliff edges it is difficult to believe a fish could survive in the roaring flow, and it seems impossible that any creature could swim upstream in it.

But the Indian, standing amid stubby evergreens which cling to skimpy plots of earth at the edge of the precipice, knows the fish are there. They are resting briefly in pockets unseen from above, pockets that might be white turbulence but can give respite to a salmon because of their lack of direction.

The Indian uses a rope to descend the cliff, taking a route he has followed many times before. His lifeline is knotted about his waist and his feet reach positively for purchase in crevices and notches that Indian feet have worn for generations.

Fifteen feet above the booming water there is a tiny platform, laboriously rigged with lines and poles, a station vulnerable to high water. From the platform the sky is a bright blue streak overhead. An occasional hawk or golden eagle appears in the slit, and now and then a gull wings its way erratically through the gorge, unsteady in air currents that reflect the course of the water.

The little platform quivers from the vibrations of thousands of tons of crashing water and spray soaks its underside. The fisherman lowers his dip net, large and coarse-meshed, made from a minimum of cordage so it will withstand the water's thrust, and he braces himself with widespread feet, his heavy lifeline slack behind him.

Fish are scarce. Earlier there had been a great run of chinook salmon, heavy fish that sometimes jerked the Indian fishermen against their safety tethers, but now it is late fall and there are only a few flashing silvers and an occasional steelhead. The excitement and labors of the main run are long past, and the Indian seeks only a fresh fish or two.

The silver has rested just below a bulging cascade that booms over a great invisible boulder, and as she prepares for a new assault she finds the exact spot where a gout of plunging water from above recoils from the rocky bottom. It is that upward thrust she must use in her half-leaping, half-swimming attempt. When she goes, her driving tail is a blur as her leap ends on the edge of the boulder's heavy burden of water, but the timing has been a little wrong and she is again swept back to the boiling hole beneath it. The watcher from the little platform has seen her dark silhouette and now he pushes his long-handled net deep and probes where he knows the fish must be, for his platform's location was not chosen by accident. Thousands of salmon have held below the great boulder and when he feels a tug that differs from the water's motion he senses the fish and swings it upward, the long pole bending as he throws his weight against it. One fish is enough for today and he works his way to the cliff edge, and then to his parked sedan a few yards away. His is an old method but the time is late twentieth century. His platform is sawmill plank and it hangs by steel cables instead of the vines and thongs of his ancestors.

It is not the Columbia itself he fishes but the Klickitat, a tributary on the Washington side. For generations his people fished the main river at Celilo Falls, but its shoals and rapids have been stilled by great dams and the long-handled nets would be useless in calm waters. Only a few of the Columbia's tributaries are now fished from stands.

At Two Ocean Pass in northwestern Wyoming, the Continental Divide, a stony spine over much of its length, becomes vague and wandering. At Two Ocean Pass there is a boggy area eight thousand feet above sea level and within sight of several ten-thousand-foot peaks. It is a good place for Shiras moose and a long way from any road. Atlantic Creek and Pacific Creek are formed in the little marshy area, one of them going down to the Snake River and thence to the Columbia and the Pacific, more than a thousand miles away. Atlantic Creek goes another way, reaching the Yellowstone, the Missouri, the Mississippi, and the Gulf of Mexico. In their beginnings both creeks have darting, hard-bodied little cutthroat trout, natives of the high country.

Pacific Creek and the rivers it joins have other fishes but the Columbia is best known as a thoroughfare for salmon and steelhead, regardless of the spawning streams they finally ascend. The salmon will run the great river, braving the pollution of cities and their industries, but their upstream trips are broken by the fish ladders, and fingerlings are battered by turbines on their way to the Pacific. Fish hatcheries along the river endeavor to replace the losses caused by man, while Pacific salmon travel the world in cans.

Silvery towers on high ridges carry power lines from the Columbia River Valley, and the smoke from sawmills dulls the river's scenery. Diesel trucks grumble with their burdens of giant logs and tugs growl at rafts of them in backwaters and on the main river. Little except the Indian fisherman on his platform is as it was before, and the fisherman is primitive in only part of his life.

2. The Endless

Supply

In the fifteenth century the inshore American waters, from the Arctic to the tropics, supported shoals of anadromous fish. The ranges of the various species so overlapped that every section of coastline had an abundance.

Atlantic salmon were found from Labrador to well down the Southeastern Coast. Striped bass moved along all of the eastern and Gulf coasts. At spawning time, shad clogged eastern rivers as far south as Florida, and the Pacific salmons entered rivers from Alaska to Southern California. There were dozens of inshore species, such as channel bass, the weakfishes, and bluefish on the East Coast, and yellowtail swung close to shore and into the estuaries of the Pacific. On the banks off eastern Canada and New England were cod and haddock. Mackerel moved in schools that might appear off any eastern beach. The offshore tuna were thick on both sides of the continent. Most ocean species were virtually untouched by North America's primitive men, for their fishing was generally confined to small and protected waters.

The Atlantic salmon's migrations actually linked America with Europe, for the fish that spawned in a New England stream might mature in ocean depths a thousand miles away. It is the same species as Europe's salmon, and it is a deep-sea fish, a big-river fish, and a brook fish. Its travels expose it to the dangers of all these waters. As a fingerling in small streams it is prey for birds and trout. As an ocean traveler it is fair game for larger fishes and animals. Its return to spawning gravels depends upon water conditions, and drought can reduce the hatch. The large number of salmon rivers was a safeguard, but the fish's habit of thronging in staging areas far at sea has been a dangerous one. The spawning population of a given river can be concentrated in a relatively small area offshore and be vulnerable to local disaster.

Atlantic salmon rivers must maintain a delicate balance of flow, purity, and temperature and are hosts to the fish on three distinct occasions. The young parr must find food and have water for passage to sea as a smolt. As a returning spawner the fish needs depth, current, and the proper bottom conformation. And as a spawned-out and weakened kelt it must have enough water to reach the sea again through the gauntlet of shoreline predators. All of these requirements were readily met in primitive America.

America's trout were completely different from those of Europe. The brook trout is not a true trout at all but a char, separated from the true trouts by having only a few teeth in the vomerine bone at the roof of the mouth. After the western trouts were identified in the early nineteenth century, it was to be called the "eastern brook trout," since its range was entirely east of the Mississippi. It was and is a fish of pure, cold waters, prospering in temperatures under sixty-five degrees Fahrenheit and perishing at more than seventy-five. Its ideal habitat is wilderness, for the brook trout lacks sophistication and is vulnerable to hazards of lake or stream that other species might survive.

The brook trout lived from Labrador west into the Hudson Bay drainages, along the Great Lakes watershed as far west as Minnesota and Iowa, and along the Appalachians as far south as Georgia. At one time in glacial history it entered the coastal streams of the South, and although a sea-run brookie remains, it is found only in the North.

It is marked by curving, wormlike vermiculation on its back, carries white fin borders and brilliant spots. Its size varies greatly with locale,

*Opening pages: Dorymen fishing
for cod—a familiar 19th-century sight along the
Atlantic Coast from Massachusetts to the
Grand Banks of Newfoundland.
Dory was a seaworthy craft, but skittish and
requiring expert handling. Man in bow
is retrieving trawl line with catch. With full
load, it will be a long pull to mother
ship or home port—and perilous if fog descends.*

and it is unlikely the first settlers found them very large, for it was in the larger lakes and in the large Canadian rivers that the fish grew to four or five pounds, and occasionally to ten. Sea-run brook trout generally average larger than fresh-water residents.

Very different trouts were seen west of the Rockies, and on both sides of the Continental Divide were the cutthroats, which probably originated on what is now the eastern slope at a time when the divide was situated differently. There were many subspecies of the cutthroat, evidently developing separately through isolation and not amenable to changes of locale. The cutthroat hybridized readily, especially with the rainbow. As with other American trouts there were seagoing cutthroats that appeared from Alaska to Southern California.

No American fish captures popular fancy as does the rainbow, a flashily colored performer of curving leaps and bold runs. It is an adaptable fish, withstanding a wide range of temperatures, living in broad rivers, mossy brooks, and blue lakes, and driving up a hundred streams each fall from the mystery of the Pacific. The rainbow displaces any less versatile trout when habitat changes and it continued to expand its range long after primitive times.

The rainbow held a special position because of its sea-run form, the steelhead, which accompanied the various Pacific salmons and was harvested along with them. Its habits closely resemble those of the Atlantic salmon and, indeed, it is believed to be a closer relative of the Atlantic salmon than of the Pacific types. The steelhead can spawn more than once, and the physical differences between sea-run fish and the nonmigratory rainbow trout are invisible, but through some subtle instinct the steelhead branch of the family seeks the sea. At sea it trades most of its crimson stripe for flashing silver, regaining its fresh-water colors when it returns to spawn. On some rivers the returning fish appear months before their spawning time in late winter or spring, a longer presence than that of most salmon.

In the West, the Dolly Varden or bull trout, a char, occupied lakes and streams from Northern California to Alaska and inland to Idaho and Montana. This fish also was known in Japan. It was not a leaper and was to gain an undesirable reputation as a salmon-egg eater, although other trout seek the eggs, too.

Arctic char were found along the coasts of northern Canada and Alaska, known only to Eskimos and Indians, and are mysterious even now because they are out of the orbit of most sport fishermen. They are found as part-time salt-water residents in cold waters of both Asia and Europe, and are represented by smaller landlocked forms, as are most other anadromous travelers. Their ocean range seems smaller than that of most salmons and they spawn in fresh water. There is a theory that the Arctic char was separated from the Dolly Varden when a land bridge divided the Pacific Ocean from the Arctic seas. In fact, their ranges now overlap in Alaska.

The ruthless shoving and gouging of the old ice masses isolated salmonoids which had evolved separately from their relatives. Some of the smaller colonies were not discovered for centuries after Columbus. The lake or mackinaw trout is a mystery, for unlike most chars, it does not migrate to sea, although it has been found in brackish water. The land bridge that once crossed Bering Strait was probably an avenue for fresh-water fishes, as well as for men and game, but the lake trout has not reached Asia. Perhaps the bridge, now covered by cold sea currents, was not suitable for the sort of deep-water habitat the lake trout requires. It must have been fairly level, a land of tundra and without deep lakes. The lake trout will spawn at a depth of a hundred feet or more if temperatures are suitable. Its native range covered most of Canada, the Great Lakes (where it was to be decimated by parasites), most of New England, and a small section of Montana. Living as deep as six hundred feet, the Great Lakes mackinaw often weighed as much as fifty pounds, making it the giant of trouts.

There were other trout isolated by changes in climate and terrain. There were some relatives of the Arctic char—the Sunapee golden was a resident of deep lakes and ponds in Vermont and New Hampshire—and there were the oquassa of Maine's Rangeley Lakes and a red trout in some Canadian lakes.

But it was in the high, rare atmosphere of the Mount Whitney area, at the head of the Kern River of California, that the steep, rocky brooks held the flickering flame and gold of the most brilliant trout of all, the high-country golden, a treasure that awaited the adventuresome. It is an offshoot of the rainbow, a violent miniature of solid flesh that darts in tiny falls between icy boulders. Because it has a rainbow's adaptability it can easily be transplanted, and when it is brought to wider waters at lower altitudes it grows larger, but the flame and gold are dimmed. Only amid the peaks does the magic hold.

Grayling became prized fish in Britain when sports angling began there, but none was available for the first settlers of eastern America. They were finally found in Michigan, dainty feeders with

Early settlers of Maine (dressing catch, above) were active fishermen. Dried and salted fish were readily traded for Virginia corn or goods from England. Harbor scene at Charleston, South Carolina, in 1739 shows fishermen at work (foreground, far left) with circular net. Fishing in 18th century was generally undertaken along shoreline or pursued in protected waters.

CATCHING BLUE FISH.

*Commercial fishermen (left) of 1875
hauling in herring net. This was hard and dangerous
work. Hours were long, seas treacherous,
men's hands were cut by nets and
hooks and stung by brine. But fishermen took
pride in their craft and, like mountain
men of West, were unbowed by
adversity. Above: Fishing for blues from
catboats, probably off Long Island.*

*Great spawning runs of Atlantic
salmon in streams of New England persuaded
early settlers that fish supply was
endless. Hired help grumbled at frequency of fish
dinners provided by employers.
Actually, salmon water must maintain a balance
of purity, flow, and temperature, and
fish themselves are highly vulnerable to attack
while thronging in staging areas at sea.*

delicate sails as dorsal fins. The Michigan grayling was a casualty of civilization, a fish dependent on the purest water and susceptible to well-presented lures, which disappeared in the twentieth century. But it was virtually the same as the Arctic grayling, which has held its own in Alaska and northern Canada. The Montana grayling is a race of the Arctic fish and is still caught in Montana, Utah, and Wyoming, but is much smaller than those found farther north. The grayling was to disappear quickly from most of its range, while the black basses spread their domain and prospered where other fishes failed.

The largemouth black bass at the outset occupied a limited range in America. There were largemouth in southeastern Canada, through the Great Lakes, and throughout most of the Mississippi Valley. There were others in Mexico and an especially large race of them in Florida, and they were found along the Atlantic Coast south of Maryland. They lived unobtrusively in backwaters of large rivers, in weedy ponds and lakes, and in sluggish streams. They lived in brackish waters along the coast, withstanding strong salinity in dry years, and sometimes mingling with true salt-water species. They made no spectacular migrations and they did not appear in large schools for the benefit of netters. In time they occupied all of the contiguous states as the most valuable sports fish of all.

The smallmouth bass had an original range confined to the Great Lakes, the St. Lawrence drainage, and the upper Mississippi, Ohio, and Tennessee river drainages. It frequently occupied the lower sections of rivers carrying trout in their swifter and colder parts, and it replaced trout if the water became too warm. Its range overlapped that of the largemouth bass; it occupied many of the same

waters, but preferred somewhat swifter currents and greater depths. It spawned on coarse gravel and cruised in the shadows of boulders. As the smallmouth usurped habitat from the trouts, so the largemouth bass has ever invaded smallmouth territories as water warms or gravel bottom is covered by mud.

The northern pike ranged across northern Asia, Europe, and North America. It lived as far south as southern New England, New York's Hudson River, the northern Ohio Valley, the Great Lakes, Missouri, and eastern Nebraska. With its evil temperament, its ambush form of feeding, and its fierce appearance, the pike was a subject of superstition more than any other fish. When a water monster was contrived in fanciful angling tales, it was almost invariably a pike, and long after fishermen had begun to understand the reproduction of other fish it was still believed the pike hatched from sun-heated pieces of waterweed. Anglo-Saxons named it after the ancient and deadly spear, and it had been called Luce, the water wolf. The pike will eat almost anything, including ducks or turtles, and when found in wilderness waters it is so easily caught that it could be a "survivor fish" for primitive travelers.

The muskellunge is somewhat different from the pike but so similar in appearance that many sportsmen thought it was the same fish well into the twentieth century. Its name comes from French and Indian words spelled and pronounced in innumerable ways. Its original American range was from north of the St. Lawrence River, through the Great Lakes area and somewhat north of there, into western New York and the Ohio River basin. It was also in the Tennessee River system and in Minnesota and Wisconsin. It was not native to Europe. In later years the musky

Fish wheel, like one below on Upper Cascade of Columbia River in late 19th century, was devastatingly efficient and eventually outlawed. Wheel was lowered into current and scooped fish into barge as fast as it could turn. It was used in conjunction with first fish canneries. Spring run of shad being hauled in (right) at Gloucester on Delaware River was also phenomenally abundant.

gained fame not only for its slashing strike but for its scarcity and difficulty. Master anglers have spent lifetimes pursuing it.

As the musky appeared to be simply a large northern pike, so the eastern chain pickerel and its little relatives, the grass and redfin pickerels, appeared to be small northern pike. The pickerel was active in cold water and was native to eastern Canada and much of the eastern United States as far south as Florida. The walleyed pike, really a perch, lived from the Mackenzie River in the Arctic, south and east to North Carolina, and to the Alabama and Tennessee rivers.

Fresh-water panfishes occupied warm waters over most of America. Atlantic sturgeon were plentiful in coastal areas near the original colonies, reaching weights of hundreds of pounds. They are anadromous fish, ascending rivers to spawn and traveling great distances at sea. They have never been considered a sport fish and suffered early from dams and pollution. The western sturgeons were long unknown.

The brackish waters of the deep South were crowded with weakfish and sometimes with largemouth bass. They served as incubators for many offshore species and supported rolling hordes of the most spectacular inshore fish of all, the tarpon. The Florida Keys and the Caribbean held their own colorful fish and were rallying areas for transient ocean species which concentrated there when their northern range was cold.

Striped bass must have been at a high point in their cycle during Pilgrim times, for Captain John Smith reported them plentiful. One of the important inshore fishes, it has fluctuated wildly in numbers, disappearing from some areas for generations, only to return in new and larger runs. Some stripers make long migrations along the coastlines, others live out their lives in a single bay, and still others have adapted to fresh inland waters.

Bluefish, as unpredictable as the striped bass in their cycles, swept the beaches in hungry shoals, frothing the bays and estuaries in slashing sprees of feeding. Shad were plentiful on the Atlantic Coast, going upstream to spawn and then disappearing at sea in untraceable migrations.

There are five Pacific salmons. Best known is the king, largest of all salmons, occasionally weighing more than a hundred pounds. Also called the tyee and chinook, the king undertakes the most dramatic journeys of any fish, not only for distance but for their incredible difficulties.

As a fingerling the tiny chinook goes downstream toward the sea in spring, preyed upon by other fishes, by wading birds, and by swimming sea birds. Sometimes the waterway it travels has been changed by flood or drought since the salmon's birth in the gravel bed of a small mountain stream. When it reaches the Pacific, the salmon travels wherever the search for food may lead, swimming perhaps a thousand miles from the home river's mouth.

*Four Great American Fish:
the beautifully colored and energetically
performing rainbow trout (right),
its sea-run form, the migratory steelhead
(below), the lively little eastern
brook trout (bottom), which actually is a
char and has both sea-going and
fresh-water types, and cutthroat (opposite),
which hybridizes with rainbows.*

At maturity, usually in about four years, the chinooks return to the waters of their birth, drawn by instinct to complete their incredible quest. It is now known that it is a sense of smell that guides them to the home stream, but their unerring routes were unfathomed for centuries.

At sea, salmon are quarry for larger fish and roving sea lions. It is as they neared the end of their journey, drawn by the spawning urge but as yet unmarked by approaching death, that they became most vulnerable to early fishermen. Some of them spend a long time near shore collecting at river mouths in preparation for the final run to their spawning gravels. When the finely conditioned salmon breast the river currents their remaining life must be precisely timed for the ordeal, and large fish in small streams are easily seen by predators.

The home river may be long. If it is the chilly Yukon of Alaska the indomitable chinook must swim upstream for two thousand miles. And whatever the river, as the waters narrow the current quickens. Streamlined fish must surmount the white rapids and smashing waterfalls, repeatedly leaping, resting after failure, and trying again. The salmon changes as it goes, red-scarred by fangs that slipped, bruised by the edged rock, and slimmed by exertion. The silver of the sea turns dark and blotched, and as the final creek is reached the gray fungus of approaching death begins to appear on the fins.

The female fish frays her fins digging a redd in which to deposit her eggs. A male hovers alongside to fertilize the spawn that sinks into the gravel, where it will be sought by small predators. There is more digging and more deposits, and at last the eggs are placed. Some newly arrived hen fish and some new males still are strong and combative, but the male that first fertilized the eggs has given way to the current, his gills working spasmodically as he disappears downstream.

The female is spawned out, but for days she continues to work erratically at the gravel, her shredded tail's final clearings hardly noticeable on the creek floor. Finally she can no longer hold against the current and slides slowly downstream, pausing to gasp in eddies over the sunken skeletons of other salmon. It is time for the scavengers, wolf and raven, gull and crow. Except that death is not always involved in its spawning run, the Atlantic salmon's life story is about the same.

There are four other Pacific salmons besides the chinook, smaller fish but with similar habits. The silver or coho was found to be a particularly sporting fish for light tackle and one day became the savior of depleted waters in other parts of the country. There is the red or sockeye, reflected in its relative, the smaller landlocked kokanee of cold lakes, and there is the humpbacked or pink salmon. In the northern salmon range is the chum or dog salmon.

THE INVADERS

European seamen of five hundred years ago were not historians, and the sketchy logs of their little ships are long gone with the wakes of their wind-beaten craft. We do not know when they first approached the North American coast.

For the earliest of those fishermen who found the cod banks off Newfoundland, however, the presence of a coastline was incidental to the business at hand and it is unlikely that they knew where they were. It may be that they fished the banks before Columbus sailed, for there are tantalizing scraps of old rumor and crude maps to indicate it.

Fishing was vital to a hungry Europe and fish cost more lives than fur or gold. Wars were fought for fish, and fishing fleets seeking new waters sailed into the unknown. John Cabot, sailing from England in 1497, visited the Newfoundland coast and reported fish being caught with nets and with weighted basket traps, presumably by Indians. Ships from France, Spain, Portugal, and England dotted the banks for centuries afterward. Thus, although the Norsemen of an earlier date had broken off their contacts with the New World, generations of European seafarers returned with the fishing fleets. Long before there were colonies tied to the land there were fishing settlements on North Atlantic coasts. They served as processing stations for European fleets, as well as bases for inshore operations from small boats.

Cabot reported that the "savages" called the cod *baccalaos*, a Basque word used by sailors from the Bay of Biscay off northern Spain, proof of earlier fishing in the estimation of some historians. Francis Parkman felt there must have been European fishermen there as early as 1450, but the first authentic record is of ships from Brittany in 1504. By 1540 the French had permanent shore installations.

The "banks" are not a continuing slope from the beaches, but submerged tablelands or plateaus separated from the shore by deeper water. Much of the banks area off the Maritime Provinces is less than three hundred feet deep, and such broad fishing bottoms could hardly be missed, even with primitive sounding methods. The Banks are more than three hundred miles by seventy-five miles.

The cod and haddock are of the same family, and the word "cod" could have meant either fish. The harvested cod commonly weighs five to twelve pounds, although there are records of a 210-pound specimen. In a later day any fish over one hundred pounds was unusual. In deep water they are found as far south as Cape Hatteras. The spawn of the cod is free-floating, and the eggs from a single female may number in the millions. The haddock is smaller, generally less than five pounds, and inclines to somewhat greater depths, although in a similar range of latitude. It has a very dark lateral line. Smoked haddock is finnan haddie.

The fishing season for European crews lasted from early June until late September, with added time required for the cross-ocean voyages. Dangers were so great that reports of those expeditions are generally melancholy accounts, stressing the sadness of overworked and sea-battered men far from home. By the time the day's catch had been processed it might be midnight, and the weary crew dined on a concoction made from codfish cheeks and called "the soup of tears." If you ate it once, the prophesy ran, you would return to the gloomy Banks again. Despite the high mortality rate among fishermen, one Frenchman is said to have fished the Banks forty times.

The earliest European codfishing ships varied as to design but tended toward the caravel type used by Columbus, with high quarterdecks and convex bows.

The more modern fishing schooner with its ricks of nested dories came much later, but small boats played an increasing part in the fishery, some of them brought aboard the ship and others based on shore. The "chalopes" were strong craft employed by the French to place "grand lines" which

held as many as five thousand hooks, but much of the fishing was with hand lines from the ships themselves.

As early as 1517, Spain had about one hundred ships on the Banks, but Spanish interests diminished as they followed other pursuits in the New World. Portugal sent about fifty ships in 1577. The English, who fished Iceland for cod somewhat earlier, had fifty ships off Newfoundland in 1522. In about 1600 the English sent two hundred ships manned by ten thousand men and boys.

The typical seventeenth-century British fishing "snow" was much like a brig with two masts, slightly more than seventy feet long and with an eighteen-foot beam. Her crew dropped anchor at her fishing station, and as she swung into position with wind and current a canvas windbreak was rigged to protect the hand-liners, who stood in large barrels lashed even with the deck. Oilskins were unknown and the fishermen wore heavy, shapeless clothing as protection against the bitter winds, stinging spray, and occasional solid sea water. Two men cleaned the fish and fed them through a sluice to a salter. Continual exposure to cold water, the cuts from lines and hooks, and the poor and irregular meals brought death by illness almost as frequently as the sea brought death by wreck and drowning. But it was such hand-lining that entertained Captain John Smith and his friends in what was probably the first American salt-water sport fishing.

The importance of fishing in the plans of the first colonists has often been overlooked in the light of events ashore, but William Bradford reported that when King James asked how the Plymouth colony proposed to further the interests of His Majesty's dominions, the simple answer was, "Fishing." The king

approved. The *Mayflower* was well stocked with fishing equipment, and there is no doubt that France's first foothold in land and furs came from rude fishing stations perched on what must have appeared a hostile coast.

At first the English colonists were ill-equipped for offshore fishing, although their early years appear to have been good ones for striped bass. They employed birchbark and dugout canoes at the outset, but eventually challenged the Canada-based French and the ships from Europe. They used caravels about forty feet long and sailed ketches in the late seventeenth century. But it was another craft that began a new era.

There is a colloquial English term, "scoon," which describes the graceful skipping of a stone over water, and when Captain Andrew Robinson's new ship came off the ways at Gloucester, Massachusetts, in 1713 it is said that someone shouted, "Oh, how she scoons!" She was a schooner and America's own, carrying iron men to the seven seas.

The two-masted, schooner-rigged Chebacco boats (named after a Massachusetts parish) were smaller, and the dogbody Chebacco was so called because of its high, square stern. Some such fishing boats carried their catches to the West Indies and returned with cargoes of molasses and rum. Another type, the "pinky," so named because of its pointed bow and stern, could make the Newfoundland journey easily and was in use in the early eighteen-hundreds. By then windmills were pumping sea water into evaporation vats at Provincetown and Gloucester to provide salt for fish curing.

Wars and rumors of war were almost continuous in the early coastal fisheries. Shore-based fishermen along the northern coast slaughtered

*Fierce northern pike (left) is a
voracious and indiscriminate feeder, but is
itself so easily caught that it may
have been a "survivor fish" for primitive travelers.
Arctic char (bottom) lives in remote
north and is rarely encountered by contemporary
anglers. It is both plentiful and beautiful.
Delicate grayling (below) needs purest water and has
nearly been wiped out by civilization.*

Indians almost indiscriminately in asserting rights to their footholds. The wars between France and England found fishermen vulnerable to death or capture. Fishing craft were often armed and sometimes escorted by warships. Shore-based fishermen sometimes fought with those from offshore ships, and select fishing sites were the cause of frequent combat. In the nineteen-seventies American fishermen still endured uneasy competition from foreign fleets.

In their way those who reached the shore and turned to face their old enemy, the sea, had the same spirit as those who appraised the inland wilderness and moved against it. The mountain man and the doryman were cut from the same cloth.

In 1850 the mother ship and its brood of dories were a romantic part of the American scene. There had been many boat-and-ship combinations before, but now it was the doryman who bore the brunt of hardships on the Grand Banks. The dory must have evolved gradually as a highly seaworthy craft, small enough to be manhandled on a ship's deck and capable of riding frightening seas under skilled hands. It was rowed, sometimes sailed, and usually carried a crew of two. Some two hundred years after it developed, sport and commercial fishermen could find nothing better for many situations. A near-duplicate runs wild rivers of the West as a "McKenzie" boat.

The doryman's job was to lay a trawl line. The term "trawl" also describes a funnel-shaped net later dragged by steam, gasoline, or diesel engine, but the doryman's instrument was a long line of baited hooks, perhaps a mile of them. It was a heavy line, suspending short, lighter stagings, sunken and buoyed. While one man rowed the other fed out the line. On short days the pickup began almost as soon as the line was laid. Boating the fish was heavy work and as the gunwales dropped closer and closer to the surface of the sea there was the possibility that a hooked halibut or another giant might overturn the wallowing boat.

The dory might have a sail, but there was no homing device. In bad weather navigation was sketchy, and although the dory is capable of riding wild seas it is not tolerant of handling errors. When nearly empty it is a skittish platform for experts only. With almost a ton of fish aboard and still five miles to go to reach his schooner's anchorage, the fisherman eyed his shrunken freeboard, felt his boat's sluggish responses, saw the wind-torn tips of waves, and watched for the swinging masts of the mother ship.

But even the sudden blow was more welcome than the cottony hell of fast-moving fog in which many dories disappeared forever. Some bankers carried cannon to signal their invisible flock. Some of them, with most of their boats aboard, weighed anchor and sailed about in what might be a fruitless search.

In the nineteenth century the American East Coast fisherman had a reputation for daring and for a deserved pride in his skills. He scorned navigational aids for the most part and sometimes took unnecessary risks in sailing small craft too close to destructive rocks. He scorned landlubbers as well, and his life was so locked into the sea that he might tell time by tide changes, rather than by the clock. Even on shore he would arrange a meeting at "low water slack," rather than by any conventional timepiece. Described as a fatalist, he was often both highly religious and superstitious. Fishermen included a share of hard drinkers and brawlers. The waterfront dive of the larger ports got its reputation from hard-bitten seamen, and the tiny fishing villages had some men of the same stamp.

The whalers were of the same breed, held in special high regard because of the length of their voyages.

The backbreaking skills of both whaler and hand-liner gained fame for some men. Among codfishermen the title of "high-liner" (fisherman with the largest catch) was treasured.

The practice of chumming became popular in the early eighteen-hundreds, and there were some who claimed they could deck a fish a second —using a jigging technique—when a school had been "raised" alongside. Baits for cod were varied according to their availability, but clams, herring, mackerel, squid, and capelin (a slender, smelt-like fish) were best known. When the usual cod bait was not available, the men fished for sea birds with baited hooks.

The powered "otter trawler," dragging its great funnel of netting, came into its own about 1920, but many cod are still taken in older ways. In the nineteen-seventies there were still descendants of the first dorymen employing similar methods from Labrador and Newfoundland south.

While the seafarers labored on the Grand Banks, early colonists with other callings fished occasionally near shore and began to learn of the shad runs and the droves of striped bass. When the Atlantic salmon were running, New Englanders waded with seines and caught them below natural obstructions in the rivers, salting wagonloads of them. And the salmon, later to be most prized of the sportsman's quarry, became a tiresome food that hirelings complained of. Menhaden, mackerel, and herring were plowed into the land as fertilizer, and it is reported that many New England cattle fed on fish instead of grain.

Although fishing was described by Captain John Smith as a pastime as well as a means of securing food, fishing for sport apparently found little favor in America until the eighteenth century, for the serious business of building a new country had little place for "idlers" with angling toys.

The great Pacific salmon resource remained untapped by commercial fishermen for centuries after the codfishermen first worked the Newfoundland banks. Although Captain Robert Gray, an American, reached the mouth of the Columbia River and named it after his ship in 1792, he reported little of the fishing resource there. It was Lewis and Clark, during their exploration that started in 1804, who detailed the fishing methods of the Northwest Indians and reported the abundance of Pacific fish.

It was not until 1839 that fish canning became feasible. The first salmon cannery, mounted on a barge, appeared on the Sacramento River in 1864. Three years later the new process came to the Columbia, and late in the century there was an influx of Scandinavian and French fishermen. A variety of nets was used and the deadly fish wheel appeared both on barges and in permanent installations. The wheel, later outlawed, turned by water power and scooped the migrating victims into containers.

Horse seining was a distinctive Columbia River method, beginning late in the nineteenth century and extending well into the twentieth. It involved towing seine boats away from the beach by powered craft and then using splashing draft teams to pull ashore the long net with its load of salmon.

When reliable gasoline engines came into use, offshore fishing with hook and line became practical, and some of the netters found there were times when it could save a bad day. Eventually, they were to take sportfishermen with them.

3. A Sport

The Macedonians of about 200 A.D. used six-foot rods and, according to Claudius Aelian, "They fasten red wool around a hook and fix to the wool two feathers that grow under a cock's wattles, and which in color are like wax." So the artificial fly was used even then. An Egyptian drawing shows a rod fisherman about 2000 B.C. The material of the rod is unknown, but there is no hint it had evolved from a spear, as some historians allege.

English fishing literature properly begins with "A Treatyse of fysshynge wyth an angle," part of an edition of *The Boke of St. Albans*, printed in 1496 by Wynken de Worde. The work is commonly attributed to Dame Juliana Berners, the prioress of a nunnery, and although students disagree as to the author, there is no question that the "Treatyse" describes a pastime which must have had a long previous history. It presents a dozen highly usable fly patterns and a well-developed rod.

The butt section described in the "Treatyse" was six to nine feet long, and the author recommended that it be of willow or rowan (European mountain ash) and evenly tapered. It should be cut in winter when there is a minimum of sap, then heated in an oven and lashed to a piece of straight, dry wood to avoid warping. The pith could be burned out, and the two tip sections could be stored inside and spliced together at the stream. Already there were ferrules of brass or iron for the butt section, but many later rods were joined entirely by cord lashings for simplicity, economy, and saving weight. Such splicings could be extemporized in case a rod broke.

The rod tip was made of two materials, the lower section of green hazel, the upper of a shoot of "blackthorn, crabtree, medlar or juniper."

The overall rod was fourteen or more feet long, which suggests that it had to be used in both hands. A metal spike or "spear" was used on the butt of many rods, employed in much the same manner as the modern surf fisherman's sand spike.

Rods remained ponderous for a long time after their description in the "Treatyse." There was no approach to really light tackle until the nineteenth century, and the first "casting" was evidently a matter of using a long staff to drop the bait or lure some distance away from shore. It was really a "pole," not a "rod," by modern standards. The "Treatyse" gave no indication that the line's weight was to be employed as in modern fly casting, and there was no mention of any sort of reel.

Very early rods often were jointed by necessity because of their great length, and the butt section was unlikely to bend either in casting or landing a fish, since it was large enough in many cases for storage of the rest of the rod in its hollowed interior. The tip, however, was somewhat flexible and likely to be fragile, so spare tip sections were needed and are mentioned in many early accounts.

Although there is no mention of a reel in the "Treatyse," there are reports that early Egyptians used a spool for their extra line. Guides or "rings" could be employed without reels, and extra line could be coiled in the hand or wrapped about something not attached to the rod. It may be that the extra line was used occasionally for casting and for playing the fish. A weighty bait could be thrown and the running line paid out as it sailed through the air. If the running line was used in that way, it was the forerunner of "strip casting," a system for throwing heavy lures with modern fly rods.

Historians have been frustrated in attempting to follow the reel's development, but they have steadfastly clung to the English literature. In 1651, there was a written report of a "wind" to be installed within two feet of the lower end of the rod. A thirteenth-century Chinese painting, however, depicts a fisherman operating from the stern of a small, high-bowed boat, using what appears to be a very short rod of two or three feet and a large-spooled reel remarkably like some of the modern instruments employed in deepwater trolling with wire line. Similar reels of various sizes can be found in other Oriental art of the period.

Lines must have begun with vines, either used whole or split for added flexibility; then there would have been woven plant fibers and some braids made from human hair. Quite early in the game fishermen turned to horsehair, twisted or braided to achieve the required strength. Hair lines were not only strong for their diameter, their visibility was very low, and hair was used well into the nineteenth century. A horsehair has a natural taper, and modern anglers have found that a single strand from a horse's tail is suitable as a leader for delicate trout fishing with small flies, although they disagree as to what sort of horses grow the strongest material.

Horsehair comes in a wide variety of colors, but the "Treatyse" deals meticulously with methods for dyeing that of a white horse to suit water conditions. The treatment materials include "small ale," alum, green vitriol, verdigris, lye, soot, walnut leaves, vegetable dyes, lime, and "tanner's ooze," the residue from a tanner's vat.

The "Treatyse" went so far as to list seasons and conditions for the various line hues. Green was for all clear water from April to September. Yellow was for clear water from September to November because it blended with weeds and grass growing in water "when they are broken." Russet was for winter. Brown was for dark water, tawny for water that was "healthy or marshy." The number of hairs needed for larger fish of different sizes was listed from minnow to salmon (fifteen hairs). Special gear for the pike included a brown-dyed chalk line and wire.

Personal hook construction was described in detail, generally beginning with square needles of various sizes, and going through processes of heating, bending, and tempering. They were to be wrapped to the line. Copper had been used for hooks, perhaps as early as 5000 B.C., and the Bronze Age began when tin was mixed with copper about 4000 B.C., the metal progressing from the Mediterranean to western Europe. Hooks were barbed and had an eye for the line. Iron began in Egypt about 2000 B.C. and there were steel hooks long before the Christian era.

During the 1600s the fishhook industry began in London and by mid-century Charles Kirby was producing a pattern that has remained in common usage ever since. Later the hook industry moved to the town of Redditch, in Worcestershire, and then to Norway, a nation depending heavily on fish and the sea. Mustad and Sons was established in 1832 at Oslo and developed an enormous array of hooks.

Leaders have ever served in one of two ways: to strengthen the tackle nearest the hook, or to make that section less visible. A primitive man with a fiber line might logically use a section of tough animal's intestine above the hook; hence the term "gut." Gut could be used for both strength and deception.

Silkworm gut is drawn from the

worm as it is ready to spin its cocoon, and there is mention of silkworm gut for fishing in 1724, but fine silk "string" had been reported more than fifty years earlier. The Swiss and the Milanese supposedly were the first to use silk gut.

The silk industry began in China and expanded to Europe, and much fly-fishing leader was made in Spain, where the quality was considered to be of the highest. Although there were repeated efforts to establish a silk industry in America, most leader material was imported. Nylon monofilament finally replaced most silkworm gut just before World War II, but some fishermen continued to prefer the traditional material. The methods of dyeing leader for special uses have continued to appear in fishing literature, and some of them are remarkably similar to the recommendations of the "Treatyse" for coloring horsehair.

The artificial jig probably developed from a primitive spearman's fish decoy, and the first "plugs" must have imitated a hooked minnow being dragged through the water. The stories of their origins are old and unproved, and often increasingly dramatic with each telling.

There is the tale of the hunter who discovered the appeal of bucktail when he killed a deer at the bank of a stream. As he dragged it away a little fluff of hair blew onto the water and a fish shot into the air with the hair in its jaws. Some versions make the fish a black bass, but the story must have been told of trout in an even earlier day.

There is the story of how Jim Heddon whittled a wooden cigar for fun and saw a bass strike as he tossed it into the water—the genesis of the first wooden plug. And the beginning of countless lure designs is attributed to the loss of various objects over-board, ranging from tie clasps to clothespins. Only the artificial fly seems to have appeared full blown, as a deliberate imitation of a living thing.

Bits of feather and hair blown by the wind are easily taken for insects, and it was natural that they be dressed on hooks and used as bait. All that was needed was a properly sized hook and material for fastening. Even the fly of the Macedonians copied the insect, *hippurus*. The flies of the "Treatyse" would be completely suitable for fishing today. They were far advanced over the tackle they were used with, and imitated some of the insects that would be copied by generations of tiers. They included three dun flies, a stonefly, a ruddy fly, a yellow fly, a black leaper, a "maure" fly, a "tandy" fly, a wasp, a shell fly, and a drake.

Hardly had Americans begun to tie flies than argument arose. Which was better, the accurate imitation of the living insect or the "attractor fly" which resembled nothing in particular but drew strikes through color, action, or flash? America was the logical place for the attractor fly to achieve great popularity because of the brook trout's gullibility when presented with garish little things.

The Atlantic salmon is taken with "impression" flies since it is not a true feeder after it enters fresh water for its spawning journey. The rainbow and cutthroat trouts, virtually unknown to anglers until about 1800, are less addicted to close imitations than is the brown trout of Europe. And the black bass, hardly recognized at first, has never been selective of pattern details, however selective it may be of action, speed, and depth.

Although "casting" as it began in the early nineteenth century was unknown, there

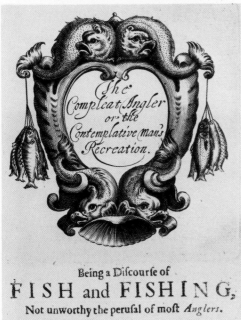

The Compleat Angler or the Contemplative Mans Recreation.

Being a Discourse of
FISH and FISHING,
Not unworthy the perusal of most *Anglers*.

Simon Peter *said, I go a fishing : and they said, We
also wil go with thee.* John 21. 3.

London, Printed by *T. Maxey* for RICH MARRIOT, in
S. Dunstans Church-yard Fleetstreet, 1653.

Sportsman angler of 1724 plays his catch
(at right, above), while commercial netters make their
haul and spear fisherman aims leister at
fat fish swimming on surface. Drawings of species
at top are highly inaccurate. Opposite:
Angler lures monstrous fish amid hawkers and
hunters in detail from Theodore de Bry's
17th-century conception of
"English Sporting Life in the New World."

is no doubt that the unwieldy early rod was capable of delicate presentation for short distances because it had complete control over its line. American fly-fishermen used such a pole, despite its short range, and many a brook trout was stalked and caught from behind streamside bushes that would have been almost impregnable for lighter rods. Early fly-fishermen, through use of a long pole, were able to gain the effect of the dry fly, although it was nearly 1900 before dry-fly fishing assembled its cult of followers. The difference was that the long pole *held* the fly on the surface when that was desired. It was not necessary for the fly to provide the delicate buoyancy that later became true "dry" fishing.

The very early American fly-fisherman of Pilgrim days approaches the stream with stealth. He is not equipped for wading since the water is very cold and waterproof waders are difficult to come by. He has studied the brook from a distance and he chooses a place where the curving current forms a logical feeding spot against a willowed bank. For this work he does not need a reel, or even line to be paid from his hand. His excess line is wrapped about the tip of his long rod and he adjusts its length by turning the rod in his hands.

In open water his rod might throw a frightening shadow, but he approaches from the willow side and carefully slides it over the low bushes and between the taller willows. There it appears as only another willow, and if its movement is slight the fish is not likely to distinguish it from other vegetation moved by the wind.

The deception may be even better if there is a brisk breeze to swing the fly delicately at the end of its tether, and the fisherman is careful to release exactly the right length of line. He can touch the fly lightly to the surface, he can dance it along, like a freshly hatched mayfly testing its drying wings, or he can allow it to sink and drift briefly, like a drowned insect. From the trout's view only the rod tip will be visible as long as the angler stands well back and peers through his camouflage, rather than over it. When the fish comes with a rush, it is lifted clear and swung back to land, and if the operation is skillful other trout will hardly notice the sudden disappearance of an associate. Within a few moments the same "cast" may be repeated with further success. Later fishermen, actually handicapped by their lighter gear, have performed the same trick when conventional casting is stymied by too much shoreline cover. If there is room, the wading fly-fisherman of today would work the brushy shore from the other side.

The old method, with long pole and short line, restricted the distance the angler could be from his lure, but its merit was that he could practice meticulous control that would have been impossible if a true cast had been made and the line were on or in the water. He had no worries about vagaries of current, and placement of his fly or lure was precise. The method has been called "dapping."

Most fishing methods evolved by traceable routes, even though the terms which describe them have changed through the years. "Dapping" often means the use of a natural fly, or flies, too delicate for the more violent motions of true fly casting. In America the word "dipping" sometimes has meant the same thing, but also has referred to the use of heavier baits that could be lowered to the pool's bottom if desired. It was a popular method for perch and other panfish.

In Britain, dapping was done from a boat, preferably on a wind-ruffled lake surface, where the popularity of natural flies continued, especially in situations where the wind could assist delicate presentations.

"Spinning," currently a term of certain definition, meant something entirely different in another century. It must have been a bait-fisherman who discovered what was then called "spinning," probably as he retrieved his minnow after presenting it unsuccessfully. It probably whirled in the water (and twisted his line), and a fish must have struck it on the way in, although it had been ignored when hanging in the water or drifting.

Later "spinning" became the retrieval of a deliberately whirled natural bait, the action being assisted by a swivel at the leader or the shank of the hook. It was the beginning of baits that did not attempt to duplicate nature, but whose action or flash provoked strikes. The hooking of the bait became a personal thing, and the bait-fish was fastened in a manner that encouraged the spinning action as it was drawn through the water. Some practitioners used other hooks trailed beside or underneath the bait. Others went so far as to pull the bait backward, with the tail bent, to encourage erratic performance—what might be termed a forerunner of the lipped casting lure.

Then there were "spinners" with an arrow-like spear for insertion through the mouth and into the body of a dead bait-fish, and shaped to improve the bait's action. The hooks trailed outside.

The "spinner" concept took still another turn with rigid, propeller-like attachments at the nose of the lure, or a tail shape which caused the whole lure to revolve. From there, it was a short step to spinners that revolved independently while the main body of the imitation maintained a level attitude or wriggled. The earliest of these commercial "minnows" in America came from England and some have survived. The American wooden plug never did completely replace the English lures. British-type minnows included the Devons, Phantoms, Proteans, and Caledonians. In Britain they were used for trout and pickerel; in America they were accepted by black bass.

Early "trolling" meant retrieving a bait with pulls and pauses. The modern definition was established in the nineteenth century, and it applied whether the angler walked along a bank or bridge, pulled on a pair of oars, or moved under sail. The spoon was an early trolling lure, its history clouded by its "invention" at various times and places. Like many later devices it was deemed unsportsmanlike by some angling authorities, the reputation affixing itself to the tool rather than the user. Thaddeus Norris called the spoon a "murderous instrument," much of his disdain arising from the fact that once it was in the water and the boat under way, the angler exerted little control over it. Hardly any game fish from pumpkinseed to billfish has not struck a spoon of some kind.

At the outset, pewter and silver tablespoons reportedly were converted to fish killers by perceptive students of angling, but the lure had more primitive beginnings than that. When Captain James Cook visited Hawaii in the 1770s he found natives using spoon lures made of shell, and spoons were still made of whole shells in the twentieth century, some of them being almost perfectly shaped for the purpose. Other materials were used with artificial "shell" finishes.

Julio T. Buel is credited with the first commercial production of the wobbling spoon. As a youth he had attracted fish with bright tin, and there is the familiar story of his invention being in-

*All-too-eager eastern brook trout was
very likely the first American sporting fish to
greet European settlers. It would have
been caught on early attractor
fly patterns, probably by "dapping,"
the English technique for dancing a lure on the
surface with a long rod and short line.
British anglers visiting colonies
were scornful of easily caught brookie.*

spired when he dropped a tablespoon from a boat. Buel entered the spoon manufacturing business in 1848 at Whitehall, New York. Considerably later, the revolving spoon which turned on a shaft was attributed to William T. J. Lowe.

Spoons were especially effective for pike and pickerel. Near the Thousand Islands of the St. Lawrence, guides rigged a rigid cedar pole, outrigger style, on either side of a skiff, running thirty or forty yards of "stout hemp line" from each of them, and attaching spoons and swivels. When a fish was hooked, the "native rod" was tipped down and the fish hauled in hand-over-hand.

Some anglers felt that natural bait was more sportsmanlike than this sort of fishing, even when they used the hook as a gorge. The time required for a fish to swallow, or "pouch," the bait was variously estimated. Some suggested as long as seven minutes, adding that as long as bubbles came from the spot where a pike was holding the bait it was not yet time to strike. "Snap fishing" was a method that involved setting the hook as soon as the fish struck and required a different hook arrangement.

Although fishing "ages" and "eras" are vaguely bordered, phases of angling development in America followed the fortunes of politics and economy.

First was the period of original exploration and settlement, a time when fishing for recreation was ignored amid the more urgent problems of survival in a new land. Once the colonies were established, wealthy Old World aristocrats visited America with time to spare for amusement. They practiced angling for brook trout as they had for European browns. Only the professional gillie was missing, an expert who served as an assistant as well as guide and performed the duties of a personal servant. There were common settlers who practiced sport fishing, of course, but they knew little of the theory of the "Treatyse" of angling or the philosophy of Izaak Walton.

When Americans declared their independence and suffered through the Revolution, they faced a period of such political and economic stress that fishing for pleasure seemed inconsequential. As the colonies became more widely separated from the mother country, the aristocratic visitors must have been rarer, and once the Revolution began, the flow of angling knowledge from Britain ceased. Students of American angling have little to report for the eighteenth century and the first part of the nineteenth.

But there was another reason for the blank pages in American fishing history. Fishing for fun was not quite respectable in puritanical society, and a sport-fishing expert might be regarded as a loafer among industrious pioneers. Cotton Mather criticized ministers who fished for pleasure in 1721. The sabbath was the only day of rest for many colonists and fishing on the Lord's day was considered sinful. It also was argued that pain inflicted on living creatures in the name of sport was sacrilege. Then a Reverend Secomb preached a sermon in 1739 to the effect that angling for sport was sinless in the sight of God. His words were widely circulated but some stigma remained. Even in the nineteenth century, authors who wrote of fishing were inclined to use pen names.

Those who did study angling in America got their background from European literature in which the status of the sportfisherman was uncertain. Hunting was approved as a warlike exercise involving some danger, a game of princes and military

*Brook trout commemorated in
19th-century oil, "Fisherman's Wall," by
Darius Cobb. In Pilgrim times,
brookie was most likely caught from shore,
since there were no real waders to
protect angler from bitterly
cold water the fish favors. Even so,
obliging trout probably made
things easy by rising quickly to take lure.*

heroes. The first English writers about fishing endeavored to make it a gentleman's sport, for people of refinement, but they did not claim it exclusively for the nobility or the rich. "Fighting" a fish, in the terminology of later record-seekers, had a small part in those early works, and the escape of a prize was likely to be treated as one of the humorous tribulations of the frustrated angler.

Izaak Walton's *Compleat Angler* of 1653 was partly a manual of method but mainly a philosophy of fishing. It depicted the angler as a contemplative person, attuned to rural settings. Angling triumphs were not heroic events, but happy interludes, leisurely enjoyments of simple pleasures with strong religious overtones. Even with less fishing it would have been a literary masterpiece.

Walton was primarily a bait-fisherman, most of his information on artificial lures being borrowed. In the fifth edition of *The Compleat Angler,* Walton's philosophical observations were joined by more technical fishing information written by Charles Cotton, his close companion on angling expeditions. *The Compleat Angler,* which has been reproduced in some four hundred editions and endlessly quoted by nearly all early fishing writers, appeared in the first completely American edition in 1847. The edition was produced anonymously by George Washington Bethune, a clergyman. Despite the nature of the work, it was thought Bethune feared censorship because of a residue of disapproval of anyone in the ministry who dealt with angling.

Cotton's how-to dissertation in Walton's edition of 1676 was a text for early American fly-fishermen, and nothing he said has been disproved by the years. Cotton was thirty-seven years younger

*Kilted Scots gentleman of 1865 has
hooked a salmon in pool below small, rocky falls.
His thick-handled rod has a
reel, but judging by his stance and grip, he
intends to derrick the fish ashore.
Patient gillie waits with gaff hook. Right:
American fishing scene appears to
date from same period. Above:
Julio T. Buel, inventor of spoon lures.*

than Walton, but evidently a close friend, a middling poet, and a mildly dissolute cavalier. His fishing was technically sound and his advice to "fish fine and far off" for trout may be the most quoted angling phrase of all time.

There are other quotations from Cotton which sound disturbingly familiar to readers of much later literature. There was a division of the water's depth into three sections—top, bottom, and middle—and Cotton gave methods for each. He firmly recommended two horsehairs for the fly line next to the hook, saying that a single hair was not enough and inferring that users of only one were pretending to be more artistic than their fellows. But he stated that anyone who could not handle a twenty-inch trout in open water with two strands "deserves not the name of angler." He recommended a tapered line for delicate casting and a one-handed takedown rod of fifteen to eighteen feet. He described sixty-five different trout

flies, listed as to the months they were to be used. Cotton was frank in stating, "I will not deny but that I think myself a master in this." He said that everyone who could afford to angle for pleasure had someone to land his fish for him.

He was a scholar and wrote on other subjects than fishing. He wrote pleasant but undistinguished verses and was a translator of Montaigne. In his time some of his poetry was considered undignified and impolite "drollery." This may be one reason why the Reverend Mr. Bethune chose to introduce his *Compleat Angler* edition anonymously (although it was a rather open secret). His clergyman's aversion to open association with fishing may not have been so great as his aversion to association with Charles Cotton!

Bethune gave Americans their own edition of Walton, but his personal fishing notes which accompanied it were strictly concerned with American conditions, however much they borrowed

*Post-Civil War fishing demonstrates
advances in techniques and tackle. Note one-handed
rods, usable reels, and multiple flies.
Below: Fly-fishing on Lake Massapequa, a private
trout preserve on Long Island. Right:
American angler and gaffer of 1875 (top), and
skittering for pickerel among
shallow-water reeds in 1865. Gaff can be seen in
boat, and flight of Canadas in rear.*

white flies were expected to catch available light, while the dark ones were to be silhouetted. Those principles remain quite valid today in both flies and lures.

Until well into the nineteenth century there were few American sportfishermen who could be termed serious practitioners. The Schuylkill Fishing Company had been founded in 1732 in Pennsylvania; evidently it was one of a number of similar organizations involved in a sort of family picnic approach. They used simple methods, generally for easily-caught fish, and seemed more interested in the convivial fish fry than in the advancement of techniques.

THE WRITERS

Washington Irving, intrigued by Waltonian philosophy, went fishing with a party of friends in an attempt to transplant Izaak's spirit in America. The result was *The Angler* (1819), a brief tale of the tribulations of beginners endeavoring to angle in a classic manner. The sketch was a forerunner of hundreds of humorous and semihumorous accounts of incompetent fishermen and their little tragedies. Irving blamed everything on geography and concluded that angling should be done in England, where there was "rule and system" and where "every roughness has been softened away from the landscape." Ironically, he complained of the very things that crowded future generations would seek, and wished for the marks of civilization that later fishermen would try to avoid.

No American sport has attracted the volume of literature that has been appended to fishing for amusement, partly because several historians seemed to consider it trivial and left it to the specialists, and partly because fishermen have tended to be writers. Hunting has been different because there is

from English theory. He dealt impartially with the matter of exact imitation versus impressionism in trout flies. Although he felt any insect was a palatable insect to a trout, regardless of color, he conceded that there were times when it was wise to attempt imitation in general color and size. His recommended flies (wet, of course) were not divided as to the month they should be used in. Much of his material gains authority through quotations from other fishermen he respected.

Bethune confessed that American trout lacked the sophistication of Britain's. His fishing, of course, would have been confined to brook trout, which never have been as selective as Europe's brown. Evidently much of his fishing had been done on Long Island, and although night fishing was not approved of in England, he thought it a choice form of American angling. The flies he mentions for night fishing were either quite light or quite dark, three flies being used together. Evidently the white or nearly

hardly any difference between sport hunting and commercial hunting. A pioneer hunted a deer for sport about the same as he did for meat, and his accomplishments were duly recorded by historians, but the most ill-informed visitor to the American frontier could see that a net was more practical than a fly or bait. Marksmanship could be applied to self-protection or conquest. A delicate cast was good for nothing except the hooking of a single fish. But it was important to anglers, and after a period of silence they loosed a flood of their own books and articles.

The fishing writer of the nineteenth century was invariably an angler himself, probably a very good one, and he became known for his expertise. Thus, a Thaddeus Norris became a hero to anglers, although probably unknown to a general public that had heard a great deal about hunters like Daniel Boone or Davy Crockett. Early angling cannot be separated from those who wrote of it. Although their work was frequently colored by English literature, they used their borrowed knowledge well in supporting their own

experiences on American waters with American fish.

American fishing history began when Dr. Jerome V. C. Smith wrote a "Practical Essay on Angling" to accompany his work on *Natural History of the Fishes of Massachusetts* in 1833. He was a fly-fisherman for brook trout on Cape Cod and for land-locked salmon in Maine. Then, in 1845, John J. Brown, a New York tackle dealer, wrote an angler's guide. It was not an attempt at classic literature, but a handbook which became widely acclaimed.

Henry William Herbert, writing under the name of Frank Forester, was the first professional angling writer on the American scene and his first book was *Fish and Fishing,* published in England in 1849 and in New York the following year. From then until his suicide in 1858 he was a leading chronicler of angling techniques, although he wrote on many other subjects. He was a strong proponent of salt-water fishing with light tackle, and he told of the thrills of striped-bass angling with a fly, a sport most present-day fishermen consider of much more recent origin.

Preceding pages: "Catching a Trout,"
painted by the noted sporting artist Arthur F.
Tait and lithographed by Nathaniel
Currier in 1854. Tackle is obviously lighter
and more flexible, small reels are ahead of hand,
ferruled sections can be seen. Angler
at left appears to have rubber boots. Weir and
earthen dam suggest an impoundment.
Below: "American Brook Trout" by Currier & Ives.

A member of a wealthy family, Herbert had been exiled from England for some mysterious reason, leaving Cambridge before getting his degree. His aristocratic background fostered his sportsmanlike approach to American fishing, but he remained an outsider to many of his readers, and some of them scoffed at what they considered his false pretensions of "gentle birth." In addition to his thorough coverage of fishing methods, Forester preached conservation and was one of the first to predict the problems that would arise from the abuse of fish supplies.

Thaddeus Norris (1811-1877) was the cheerful author of *The American Angler's Book* (1864), which came nearest to the philosophical approach of Walton. This was not only a technical manual for anglers; he pictured the sportsman often in a contemplative mood, and he was humorously critical of other angling writers' snobbery.

His chapter on "The Angler's Sabbath" was not an essay on religion, but a description of those things a fisherman could enjoy in a rural setting without a rod in his hand. Students of angling literature still list his lengthy volume as required reading.

No ruse of trout fishing has received more attention than the dry fly, its development being attributed to a list of anglers ranging from users of the Florida bob to the polished performers of English chalk streams. There is no thought that Norris invented the dry fly, but he certainly reported a method of fishing a fly in a dry manner. That is, the flies were not tied specifically to float, but he makes a point of fishing them on the surface. It was simply a matter of switching them dry between casts and delivering them lightly so they could stay on the surface for a time, giving fish a chance to take, before sinking or being drawn under by line or current. Such tactics were recommended only for very gentle flows. It was customary to fish at least two flies: a stretcher at the end of the leader and a dropper or two farther back.

Norris described true fly casting, using the weight of the line to gain distance, and he said the fly should alight before line or leader although he conceded that could not be managed on long throws. He thought it best to have the line and leader sunken while the fly was floating. Whether such angling is true dry fly-fishing, it achieved the same results.

"Uncle Thad" did not pretend to have originated these fly methods, but reported how he had watched others using them. He was not an exponent of exact duplicates of insect life, pointed to the effectiveness of "attractor" patterns, and mildly disagreed with English authorities and their "strict imitation."

Angling writers of the period were bitterly critical of each other and did not hesitate to name names or attack the backgrounds of their competitors. And while they endeavored to build American codes of angling, they often showed the thrust of English traditions, especially in judgment of their fellow anglers.

Charles Hallock (1834-1917), the founder of *Forest and Stream* magazine in 1873, is known for books on the angling of his time, emphasizing the where-to-go theme as American fishermen began their wanderings to distant waters. Scholars speak kindly of his writing. When others were critical of J. J. Brown, the handbook author, Hallock defended him with broad sarcasm, saying that Brown was "only a poor tackle maker without classical education or social position and how could he be expected to know anything?" Hallock's work appeared through most of the transition period from the beginnings of light tackle to truly modern methods and equipment.

Dr. James A. Henshall (1844-1925) has a special niche because of his approach to the black bass, an American fish taken by distinctive methods less traditional but as scientific as any procedure devised for trout. Concerning the black bass, he wrote his best-remembered words: "ounce for ounce and pound for pound, the gamest fish that swims." The "Henshall rod" was a forerunner of modern bait-casting rods, and although it was designed primarily for the use of live bait, it was only a step away from plug-casting equipment. The precision Kentucky reel, coupled with developments from Henshall's rod were the basis for bass fishing which actually pushed the bass fly rod into the background.

Other helpful writers of the nineteenth century include Genio Scott, who wrote *Fishing in American Waters* (1869) and lamented ruthless poaching; Robert B. Roosevelt, who wrote *Superior Fishing* (1865) and was deemed pompous by his contemporaries; W. C. Prime, a teller of colorful stories, who wrote *I Go A-Fishing* (1873), and George Dawson, whose *Pleasures of Angling* appeared in 1876.

There were many nineteenth-century magazines and newspapers which used angling material and some of them had complete angling departments. Best known of the early ones was New York's *Spirit of the Times,* which began in 1831 and was a vehicle for most of the fishing writers of the day. Until the Civil War the *Spirit* used fishing articles and letters regularly, and its yellowed columns furnish a running account of developments and discussions.

There were many master anglers whose efforts were unrecorded, but without the angling writers there would have been no record at all.

4. Educated

Thumbs

No one knows when the first black bass was caught by a white man, but there is little likelihood he knew or cared that it was an undiscovered fish. The Spaniards must have encountered largemouth bass in the South, and the first black bass caught by English settlers in New England was probably a smallmouth. And although there is little record of it in angling literature, the cavaliers of tidewater Virginia and Carolina, fugitives from English civil war, were bass fishermen—probably in the classical manner as befitting gentlemen of aristocratic birth.

When later fishermen admired the basses' strength and willingness to strike baits and lures on sporting tackle, it was natural to classify the fish with the much-admired trouts and salmons, and then with the true basses, such as the salt-water striper. Its common present name of bass overruled later taxonomists, who found it to be a sunfish.

The largemouth, eventually to become the premier game fish of all, appeared on the scene in a series of rumors, confused with the smallmouth and receiving an even longer list of local names. A hundred and fifty years after smallmouth and largemouth bass began to be separated in the eyes of fishermen, taxonomists isolated differences in fish from widely separated areas and began to classify them.

The classification of black basses had a poor beginning. Since France was the major center of scientific ichthyological research, it was natural for specimens to be sent there for study in the early nineteenth century. Unfortunately, the first individuals were deformed, just nontypical enough to produce incorrect counts of fin spines and to deceive the French experts as to structure.

The wide variety of fish colors due to water conditions contributed to improper classification, as did the confusing desire among the various "discoverers" to affix new scientific names, especially names that would honor the researcher. All of this came two hundred years after the time the bass must have first been caught by settlers.

Smallmouths, generally of fairly dark color, became "black bass" in the common angler's parlance and the term "Oswego bass" was one of the first names for the largemouth. More than twenty names appeared, largely of a local nature. Some of the early ones disappeared from common use, but continue to surface in widely separated communities even today.

"Growler" was one of the most confusing names used to designate largemouth bass, but the historian finds that some fishing writers used it to describe the smallmouth. In the South, where true fresh-water trout were scarce or lacking, the bass was persistently referred to as a salmonoid. There are still localities where the largemouth is a "green trout."

Confusion was heightened where both largemouth and smallmouth were found in the same waters, especially where the lower reaches of smallmouth rivers slowed and warmed to fit the other fish's requirements. Local names continue to change with new generations of fishermen. Where the smallmouths were "black bass" and the largemouths "linesides" as recently as 1930, the smallmouths became "brown bass" or "brownies" by 1960.

The pioneer brook-trout fishermen must have been introduced to smallmouth bass as he went downstream from cold mountain brooks. Where the water of rocky streams became too warm for trout the smallmouth prospered and probably surprised the angler with violent attacks on trout baits or flies.

*Opening pages: Varney split-bamboo
bass rod with B.C. Milam "Kentucky" multiplying
reel rests on copy of* Forest and Stream,
*the leading sportsman's magazine
of midcentury America. Milam was watchmaker and
partner of Jonathan Meek, who
produced first Kentucky reels commercially. Great
contribution of Kentucky was
precision that made casting from reel practical.*

But the smallmouth most likely was an incidental catch for a man more interested in trout. He may have used somewhat larger ties when he really expected bass. The first fly-fishing expressly for bass is generally credited to early settlers of Kentucky, people of British ancestry who brought fly tackle with them to their new home. James Henshall credited J. L. Sage, a Frankfort, Kentucky, reelmaker, as the first man to take up serious fly-fishing for bass; Sage had a rod and reel especially intended for this purpose in 1848. Actually, however, Kentucky is better known as the birthplace of the bait-casting reel.

KENTUCKY REELS

The grackle teeters on a bent spike of reed, his clucking commentary changing to mild alarm as a broad lily pad twitches sharply inches below him. A moment before, the bird had been standing on it searching for bugs about its edges, but when the minnows showered he hastily sought a higher perch.

The little storm of frantic fish leaves a spatter of circles, and as the school disappears a few laggards glint in the sun. A little green heron, his fierce eyes intent on the minnows, hurries along a bank of half-floating vegetation and then stops uncertainly, apprehensive of whatever has moved the bait.

The strike comes as a boiling chug at the surface, not at the tiny minnows but at some larger victim that has been pushed from beneath the pads. The smaller fish shower again.

The fisherman's skiff is guided gently with oars, but the light breeze moves it along the indistinct shore and the angler sees the strike and the moving bulge that follows. The native cane rod is more than ten feet long, not too far removed from those that are used to dip heavy baits from shore, but the reel is of gleaming workmanship and the angler's thumb contacts its spool firmly as he measures the distance to his target area.

His minnow bait is carefully hooked near its dorsal and the cast is made with a smooth swinging motion from the side, much different from the wrist snap that will prevail in later years, but the thumb plays expertly on the whirling spool and the wet, raw-silk line gives off a little haze of moisture as the bait sails to its mark. It sinks quietly and the angler picks up his rod tip gently to make sure his bait is not tangled in the pads. Then there are short, quick movements of the line where it enters the water, evidence of darting movements by the frantic bait, and a surface swirl from the heavy fish that has approached it.

When the line begins to move off steadily the fisherman gives slack, pulling coils from the reel to lessen the resistance. The line stops for a few seconds and then begins moving again. The fisherman strikes briskly and the bass comes out of the water. It is a heavy fish. Its wide-open mouth shows first just above the surface, moving from side to side with the thrusts of the submerged tail as the bass gathers for a leap. And then it goes straight up, exposing its entire length and falling back in a white-frothed splash that brings exclamations from the grackle. The green heron flies away. The angler bows his rod to pull his prize toward open water. The butt is thrust against his body to counteract the fish's leverage on the long rod. It is a beginning of true bait casting and the fisherman uses a "Kentucky reel."

Before the multiplying Kentucky reel, the "running line" or "strip-casting" technique used with a cane pole was effective for delivery

*Brook trout (brilliantly depicted by
Winslow Homer) was favorite eastern fish transplanted
to cold western waters. Rainbow replaced
them elsewhere. Below: Meek bait-casting reels.
Top two are 1845 models handmade by
B.C. himself. Four below date from 1890 to 1940. Farthest
right is rare level-wind. Bottom: Page of
fishing necessities from early catalog, and "The
Happy Moment" by James G. Clonney.*

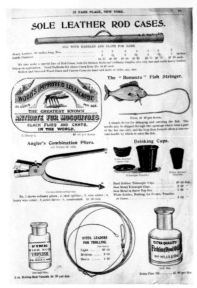

BASS — FISHING.

of a live bait for short distances, but it involved coiling line in the hand and releasing it as the rod swung forward. Although a reel was almost essential for such work, it was mainly utilized for line storage and as a windlass for playing fish. A simple drum was sufficient.

The Kentucky reel began a completely new concept, not only because it was a multiplier, but because it offered precision that made casting from the reel practical. The first Kentucky reel is credited to George Snyder of Paris, Kentucky, between 1800 and 1810, when little of the angling world knew that the black bass even existed. Snyder was a watchmaker and silversmith, and his reel was a quadruple multiplying instrument, the same gear ratio that was maintained as fresh-water casting technique advanced. All of those first Kentuckys were custom-made and quite expensive. Snyder, a member of an angling club, constructed them only for himself and his friends, and never aban-

doned his other work. Jonathan Meek, another watchmaker, produced reels commercially, however, so his product is better known than Snyder's.

Snyder built one of his reels for Munson Brown, a Kentucky judge living at Frankfort, and when it was stolen in about 1833 Brown had Meek build a reel similar to the Snyder model. Jonathan and his brother, B. F., became partners in 1840 and divided their building into separate sections for watchmaking and reel manufacture. The early Snyder reels had pillars riveted to the baseplates and the other ends secured by wire. The spool shaft protruded from the endplate in most cases. Early Meek reels had clicks and drags engaged with sliding buttons but not readily adjustable. B. C. Milam, a Meek apprentice and later a partner, improved the reels, as did J. W. Hardman of Louisville, who introduced screws for easier dismantling. Meeks of about 1845 were assembled with num-

Fishermen took a long time to identify
bass species, but they soon learned that in warmer
waters, below the brookie's mountain
streams, there were hefty fish which attacked flies
or bait with equal violence.
Here an angler wielding the long rod most
frequently used with Kentucky
reels hooks a willing fighter, probably
in a southern lake in 1860s.

bered screws. Years later there was a trend to a simple takedown, a widely advertised feature. Most of the earliest casting reels were of brass with square steel gears, which Meek began to bevel about 1860. Nickel or German silver appeared after the Civil War.

Spool shafts later were enclosed in housings, and jeweled bearings were added to make turning smoother. Many of the finer models had sapphires. After the Civil War large Kentucky reels went to salt water, but coastal users wanted double multipliers rather than quadruples.

Great rod length was believed necessary for early casting, even with the free-turning Kentuckys. The typical jointed Kentucky rod was made from about ten feet of cane, and reels were attached by lashings, or with screws through the baseplates. These rods were quite light, weighing less than salmon fly rods, and when bait-casting rods were shortened they were made from heavier woods, probably gaining in casting qualities what they lost in delicacy. The notion was that once the bait was a long distance from the rod tip, the rod's action was no longer so important in its manipulation.

It was natural for bait casting to begin in Kentucky. Many of those who practiced it were wealthy landowners and professional men who might have devoted themselves to trout or salmon had they lived in a different setting, and they wanted the best equipment. Although they led in fly-fishing for bass, there was a mysterious pause in the development of bait casting that continued for seventy years. From the time of the long Kentucky cane rod, through the shortened Henshall rod, and up to the "Chicago rod," there seemed to be little use of artificial attractions with the casting reel. It could not have been for lack of lures,

for the spoon was available, as were British artificial minnows. But serious artificial-lure casting awaited development of the American plug.

Bass tackle also seemed to be isolated by geography. While Kentucky cane rods were as light as four to six ounces, there were heavy poles in use elsewhere for generations. A Wisconsin fisherman and tackle dealer stated that in 1861 he had forsaken tamarack poles for rods which he ordered from New York. They were fifteen feet long and weighed nearly one and one-half pounds.

Dr. James Henshall described the "coming black-bass rod" in the seventies, and then introduced the rod that was to bear his name. He described the American trout fly rod as an ideal to be approached in weight and balance, and believed that the bait rod should match it in feel. The result was an instrument with very precise specifications. The Henshall rod appeared in a variety of materials, but his original specimen had a butt of white ash and other sections of lancewood. He reported making casts of fifty yards with it under favorable wind conditions. The rod was eight feet three inches long, and in feel it was a close match for the "typical" ten-foot trout fly rod. It was necessarily much stiffer, however, so it had to be shorter to match the fly rod's weight.

The Henshall rod was a breakthrough and the revolution would not stop, for after accepting the "short, light" Henshall rod for a time there were those who, in Henshall's own words, would "out-Herod Herod." The rods became still shorter and then reached a point that Henshall felt destroyed their sporting qualities. Long and pliant rods had been emblems of sportsmanship. These shorter casting rods, used with brisk forward motions instead of a sidearm

Two notable artists deal with the black bass. A.B. Frost depicts fisherman of 1882 bringing quarry to boat within reach of netter. Catch cannot be seen, but depending on local custom and usage, it could be a smallmouth, or largemouth like gaping leaper in Winslow Homer watercolor at right. Great fish has risen swiftly to bright streamer fly and been hooked in lip.

sweep, began to approach modern casting technique for artificial lures, and the "Chicago rod" appeared to lead the trend. It was stiff, a typical model being about six and one-half feet long, and was especially good when using frogs in weedy water. To the Henshall rod it was very nearly what the Henshall rod had been to the trout fly rod, giving a similar feel in spite of its short length. Equipped with a multiplying reel it was capable of landing a bass with dispatch, a quality not admired by those who felt that playing a fish was the final measure of "scientific fishing." There would be a similar objection to specialized bass tackle nearly a hundred years later. After the Chicago rod became popular about 1890, artificial bait-casting lures also caught on. James Heddon is said to have invented his plug in 1896.

Black bass are considered among the more intelligent of game fishes and part of their appeal is in the vast array of equipment used to capture them, for at some time and place the bass has been taken with almost every artificial lure ever invented. As biologists started to study fish behavior, sportsmen began to set qualifications for worthy game fish, and one of the common demands was that the subject strike an artificial lure. This the bass did especially well, although American fishermen gave it little chance to do so (except for flies) for nearly three hundred years. Bass also jumped when hooked—another qualification in the opinion of some.

Then, crediting the fish with rather complex mental processes, fishermen decided that the black bass would strike out of anger. There seemed no other explanation for its spirited attack on

flashy lures that bore no resemblance to living creatures, and brilliant colors seemed to work especially well. There were long arguments as to whether fish could actually detect colors, and the gaudy lures were used for some time before scientific proof was available that they could.

But distribution was the main factor in the black bass' popularity, and despite local names and wholesale confusion of largemouth and smallmouth the fish was soon recognized in all the United States. The black bass was a railroader. Everywhere rails went down the bass soon followed, sometimes introduced by the railroad companies themselves, but often as a casual bucket passenger borne by someone who felt this fine fish deserved to see new waters. Before the railroads, any introduction was complicated

by the rigors of travel, but once the trains were running it was possible to go many miles without even changing water on the fish.

The railroad was the only quick route from the city to distant fishing water and the industry made the most of it. Railroad companies pushed their own stocking programs, advertised in sporting publications, and offered records of their stocking programs to traveling sportsmen seeking new hunting and fishing grounds. The railroads and the bass also cooperated in other ways.

The huffing wood and coal burners had to have water for their steam boilers, and as broad-backed immigrants pushed the ringing steel into prairie sunsets, they left tanks and "railroad ponds" in their wake. Railroad ponds were among the first im-

poundments built in the name of power. Only the waterwheel dams of the eastern mills preceded them. They were simple affairs, located where likely streams could furnish water and spaced to match the appetite of thirsty locomotives. The railroad grade itself often made up the dam and the spillway went under the rails. Now there was water and possibly a resident attendant for the pump. A tank town was born.

The pond itself was a basin from which earth had been scooped for the grade. The water was backed up to cover a few acres of grassland. Soon it attracted a border of willows, a band of lily pads, water grasses, and strips of cattails. Thereafter mallards and teal swept in during fall and spring, or nested during summer if the pond were far enough north. The bass would have come with the rails, probably accompanied by pickerel and possibly by pike. Fertile, newly-drowned land would produce a crowd of bass, plus sunfishes and catfish, all of them readily washed over the spillway and into downstream creeks.

Finally, the railroads spread fish in another way. When strip-mining scarred the land to provide coal for the locomotives, deep pits were left to nurture yet other colonies of bass and panfish.

It was not only in man-made waters that traveling bass succeeded. At first only a few naturalists noticed the effects of lumbering and farming on trout streams. Fallen timber left gaps through which the sun reached shallow brooks and warmed them beyond the tolerance of brook trout. The brookie, capable of prospering in trickles of snow water where minimal food was available, required a maximally clean environment. It could live in the forest-rimmed mill ponds of eastern hills and even grow to great size there, but whenever waters warmed the brookie faded.

The bass was introduced in such places, often with great success, but to the displeasure of anglers who considered it a rough fish. Even now there is bitter denunciation of both large- and small-mouth bass where they are considered competitors of trout, and many New England anglers have refused to accept them. Fish culturists soon learned they could

Biggest game fish other than Atlantic
salmon was muskellunge of the Great Lakes and the
Thousand Islands of the St. Lawrence River.
Difficult to catch and persistently
confused with northern pike, the musky was fished by
trolling spoons—the first artificial
lure popularly used—from a double-ended rowboat.
Angler here has dispensed with
niceties and is handlining his catch to boat.

not turn back once they had meddled with unforgiving nature, but there are many waters where bass and trout, or bass and landlocked salmon, live together. Generally the bass is dominant. It can live successfully with both white and yellow perches.

At first the largemouth bass was primarily a shallow-water species, found in lakes and rivers with many obstacles and much vegetation, living in cover which provided both protection and ambush. The smallmouth was often in the same or similar habitat, but held also in more open water, preferring rocky shores and able to tolerate swifter currents. Both fish spawn in nests or "beds," the largemouth preferably in shallow areas, seeking sandy spots in muddy lakes. The smallmouth is basically a deeper gravel spawner, and although both lay their eggs in cleared spots they do not dig redds as do salmon and trout. Several females may leave their thousands of eggs in the same nest.

As in the case of the salmons there was apprehension regarding the consumption of spawn by other fish. Small panfish, especially the bluegill, were found to take bass eggs, but it was also known that small sunfish provided an important part of bass diet. Overcrowded panfish resulted in stunting and often a dearth of bass—an uneasy relationship that is not completely understood today.

Early bass fishermen believed the fish hibernated in cold weather and thus were able to survive in their northern range, but later research showed that the fish, although feeding little, do not become completely dormant, and modern fishermen take bass at times when old methods would have failed.

POACHERS AND PRESSURES

While the black bass covered the nation there were troubles with other sporting fishes. The trout streams of the East had begun to suffer from heavy fishing pressures, lumbering, farming, and stream pollution. Commercial fishing lacked regulation and wild trout were sold openly.

By 1850 the salmon angler was finding it necessary to travel far for his sport. Brown, the tackle merchant and fishing writer, said that steamboat traffic had interfered with salmon runs in the Hudson and Connecticut rivers and that the fish had been "driven farther north." Actually, the spawning salmon of the more southerly streams were disappearing and shad runs were decreasing.

Hook-and-line anglers became critical of commercial fishermen, often with good reason, and poachers had become a problem in small trout streams. Well along in the nineteenth century there were rural areas of Long Island with highly productive brooks, and being close to large fish markets they were prime targets for illegal operations.

Poachers studied the water by day, learning where trout were plentiful by cautious observation from high banks, and then returned at night, usually in pairs. A raid on a pool was the work of a few moments and was executed with fine-meshed silk seines which could be easily concealed under a coat. With a man on each end the drag was performed briskly and with little commotion, and since it was done during the open season for hook-and-line fishing the catch could be in a fish market the next day.

Angling codes were subjected to acid criticism in books and magazines, most fishing writers condoning only hook-and-line methods. Salmon spearing fell into disfavor, although spears were accepted in much ocean angling. Overly heavy fresh-

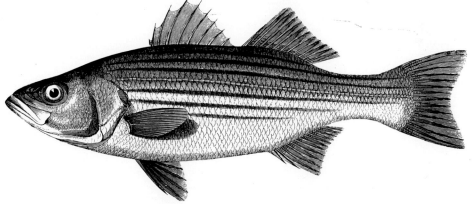

*Surf-fishing from rocks or artificial
"stands" like that at top was sport of elite anglers
from end of Civil War to 1900.
Prize quarry was the mighty striped bass, also known
as rockfish (above), which could
top 50 pounds. Casters claimed unbelievable throws
of 100 yards with long rod and
knucklebuster reels. Left: Conroy salt-water
reels of 1845–58 and striped-bass rod.*

water tackle was considered equipment for boors, but there was little talk of returning fish to the water until late in the century. The barbless hook was a satisfactory means of catching fish to be used for propagation, and then became a mark of sportsmanship once the catch-and-release concept began to appear.

The obvious depletion of game fish aroused interest in fish husbandry, and Seth Green became the "father of American fish culture." Green, born in 1817, was a lifelong resident of Rochester and once known as "the laziest boy in town" because of the hours he spent observing fish in the Genesee River. He conceived the idea of propagating fish artificially while watching spawning salmon in Canada, and his studies were responsible for the beginnings of modern fish hatcheries. Green had only a common school education but he was a practical man. He had observed the loss of spawn in natural reproduction and determined that drastic reduction of the proportion of water to milt improved the hatch. In about 1864 he laid the foundations for the New York state fish hatchery at Caledonia. He already owned trout ponds there.

His success with shad was spectacular. When he went to Holyoke, Massachusetts, to experiment with them in 1867, professional fishermen opposed him, even destroying his nets, but he invented a hatching box and quadrupled the natural output of the Connecticut River. Later he was successful with propagation in the Hudson, Potomac, and Susquehanna rivers, dealing with fifteen different species of fish. In his lifetime he hatched twenty species of fish and produced several hybrids. He introduced the American shad to the Pacific Coast in 1871. He served with Robert B. Roosevelt and the former governor, Horatio Seymour, on the New York State Fish Commission.

He was an accomplished sports angler and writer.

His contemporary, Louis Agassiz, the Swiss naturalist, was a scholar of classification rather than of propagation, and as an educator did much to clear up the jumble of facts and rumors about American fishes, especially those of salt water. Although he had previously studied and taught in the United States, he did not become a citizen until 1865. He attracted generous grants for his later study and made numerous research voyages, including a study of the Florida Keys. Like some other scientists, he used the Fulton Fish Market as a laboratory; in his day it was a showplace.

An official beginning of fish conservation on a national basis came with creation of the United States Fish Commission by Congress in 1871. Its purpose was to investigate conditions and causes for the decline in the sea fishing of southern New England and the whitefishing of the Great Lakes. Such a body was badly needed in view of indiscriminate stocking practices, and although many mistakes were made it was a beginning of cooperation between states.

SPORT AND THE SEA

Offshore salt-water angling began slowly. Really large fish were virtually untouched until nearly 1900. "Scientific angling" was the common term applied to light tackle on fresh water, but offshore fishing was either robust adventure or commercial labor.

Where larger fish were concerned the spear or gun was acceptable, and Charles C. Ward described hunting porpoises with Indians in the Bay of Fundy in 1883. It was a sort of miniature whale hunt with Passamaquoddy Indians who sought the porpoises for oil as well as meat. As far as two miles offshore the Indians hunted in birchbark canoes with sails. Their procedure was to shoot the porpoise with a smoothbore musket and large shot and then finish it with a spear, after which the hunter hauled the heavy victim aboard by hooking his fingers in the blowhole. Porpoise oil brought a high price. It was in demand by watchmakers and for lubricating heavy machinery, and remained satisfactorily fluid in very cold weather. That was not properly angling, but it was sporting and dangerous.

It was the fresh-water angler who brought sporting tackle to the ocean and to some degree he was led there by two special fishes with very different things to offer. The striped bass met him in fresh-water rivers, where he used trout or salmon gear, and coaxed him by degrees to the crashing surf. The tarpon awed him at first, but tantalized him because it remained available, within easy reach of skiff or canoe, and he could not resist the challenge. When he had planned for these two fish and their near neighbors, he found he had planned for the seven seas.

Fly-fishing for striped bass began very early and by the end of the Civil War the salmon rod and fly were popular on the Potomac, near Washington. Robert B. Roosevelt, who classed the striper second only to the salmon as a game fish, especially when caught in swift water, reported that a large hook and any showy fly was satisfactory, although using a float and paying out downstream line was less refined than classical casting.

It was the "ignorant and debased natives" living near Tenally Town by Washington whose fly-fishing enraged Roosevelt. They used peeled cedar saplings with stout cords and wrapped strips of red or yellow flannel about large hooks. Crawling out

Surf-fishing for bass in 1903. Casters became experts at reading rips, eddies, and pockets of boiling water at ocean's edge. They used up to 300 yards of oil-soaked linen line and double multiplying reels, and were often drenched by breakers for their pains. Sport was ending about this time as stripers mysteriously left northeast coast, not to return until 1936.

Wild-eyed bluefish (right) by Arnoud Wydeveld is hooked on tin squid, probably in midst of a feeding fury. Blues running with stripers often destroyed surf-fishermen's lines and leaders, and were more readily caught by handliners trolling from catboats. When blues were schooling, a skipper who could get bait to the fish was guaranteed a fine catch.

Long considered impossible to catch
with rod and reel, the tarpon was finally
conquered in 1885. Part of the answer
was better tackle, part learning to let fish run long
enough to swallow bait and set
hook. After that, 100-pound catches became common.
Lithograph (bottom) shows still-rare
catch of 1889. String of stripers
(right) is by Henry Mount Smith, about 1831.

on projecting rocks they fed their "miserable flannel abortions" into swift current and took fish of twenty pounds. The author states that some of the "stupid boors" fell from their slippery perches, occasionally with fatal results, but he did not consider the method sporting at all.

Fly-fishing for striped bass was good at several spots on the Potomac, as well as on rivers farther south, but at that time there was little fly-fishing in the North. In southern rivers, and occasionally to the north, a full-bodied red and white fly was productive when fished in narrow inlets where fresh water met the salt. Salmon fly rods were also used with shrimp as bait.

Eel skin, taken from the tail section of the eel and sometimes salted for preservation, was generally used with a hand line in Roosevelt's time and cast into the surf. Trollers often used metal lures. Surf-fishing from rocks or artificial "stands" with casting equipment took some of the largest bass and attracted wealthy anglers who organized their own exclusive bass clubs. Those clubs began shortly after the Civil War and thrived until 1900, when the fish unaccountably disappeared from the New England coast and was not seen again for thirty-five years.

Some good casting spots were simply strategic promontories from which a caster could reach promising water, but the man-made stands were a refinement. The typical stand was mounted on steel legs set in holes drilled in shoreline boulders and was a miniature of the fishing piers of a later day—the wooden platform, usually with a bench near the ocean end. During the off-season the platforms could be removed to avoid storm damage and most of them were simply made to offer a minimum of resistance to the waves which frequently broke over them.

For the most part the bass clubs that brought stand-fishing to its peak were made up of wealthy and prominent New Yorkers. They built comfortable clubhouses, hired staffs of gaffers, chummers, and clubhouse attendants, and kept contact with their city offices by carrier pigeon. And although their substantial catch was sold and the receipts applied against bait costs, there was seldom a profit. Chumming in the grand manner was expensive.

Club members lived a good life in their headquarters, where food and drink were the best, but stand-fishing was not a game of luxury. The stands were designed to keep the fisherman above high tide level, but when the surf ran tall (often the best time for bass fishing) there was whipping spray and the angler's feet might be under water part of the time. When the biggest combers arrived, marching in their traditional triumvirates, there were times when the angler clung to his bench, held his breath, and disappeared in cold sea water. There were stories of elderly Seth Green tying himself to his stand and hidden intermittently under breaking waves.

The reels used by surf-casters were later to be called "knucklebusters," since they did not free-spool, and the fishermen used thumbstalls, or "cots," of leather or rubber for snubbing the fish's run, as well as for controlling the cast. The most proficient of the bassers wore a stall on each thumb, for they learned to cast with whichever hand was practical at the moment. Rod lengths varied, but they were not extremely long, and carried two to three hundred yards of line, generally on double multiplying reels. The stand fisherman had to play his catch without following it and the fish might weigh fifty pounds or more.

Early 20th-century bait-casting
gear, primarily for black bass, but also suitable
for pike, pickerel, or muskellunge.
Grips are straight, not offset.
Reel on cork-handled rod has jewel bearing. Lures
are bass plugs with spinning
elements. One at left has attractive streamer
and multiple hooks. Shakespeare
was a well-known manufacturer of tackle.

Although the chum sometimes brought fish to close range, the adept caster could throw nearly a hundred yards and some claimed as much as a hundred twenty under favorable conditions. (Later experts did not believe such distances possible.) A variety of natural baits was used. Carefully rigged menhaden was a favorite. Anglers of the day were pleased with their American-built rods and reels, but continually sought better lines. Some soaked linen lines in fish oil and drained them before use. Oil helped prevent soaking by salt water, but at best the lines were highly perishable. Bluefish were seldom welcome in the chum slick for they often cut lines just when bass fishing was at its best.

Much of the fascination of surf-fishing was and is fostered by the powerful "rock fish's" feeding forays in the boiling troughs and in the very curl of building breakers. Although striped bass can be caught from boats in calm seas and from the solid footing of sod banks on inland bays, it is its love for moving water that appeals to the angling adventurer, who learns to read the boiling rips, sweeping eddies, and rocky pockets. On a larger scale he studies his water as does a trout or salmon fisherman, while the sea changes constantly with tidal current and shifting winds. No fisherman becomes more learned or addicted.

The old club names included Cuttyhunk, Squibnocket, Pasque Island, West Island, and Cohasset Narrows in the vicinity of the Elizabeth Island chain, off the Massachusetts coast. The Providence Club was made up mainly of Rhode Islanders. Writers of the day recommended that enterprising bass fishermen buy shares in such clubs, but not every angler could afford it or gain admittance.

The bass, addicted to patterns that change through periods measured by decades, almost abandoned New England shores about 1900. The steel supports rusted away and a way of fishing disappeared. In 1936 the bass came back, and even Frank Woolner and Hal Lyman, sachems of the high surf in a later day, could not say where they had gone.

While the bass clubs were at their zenith, striped bass from New Jersey traveled to San Francisco Bay in railroad cars, their primitive tanks agitated by hand and the water changed at intervals. The importation was successful and new arrivals spread along the Pacific Coast to stay. Less heralded than the northern fish, the striper also was found on southern coasts of the Atlantic and the Gulf of Mexico, and much later it was a prize in inland lakes. It sweeps the coasts in mass seasonal migrations, not always predictable. It lives in stay-at-home colonies about estuaries, and its spawn floats free in moving fresh water. It is a powerful fighter of stubborn runs and throbbing soundings on straining tackle, and its detractors can only say, "It doesn't jump very much."

Striped-bass anglers have often been bluefishermen as well, the two species often being found together, and the bluefish has long been taken with artificial lures, bone or metal contrivances that have little resemblance to living things but are fiercely struck during feeding orgies. The same lures work for striped bass in nickel, pewter, or glowing solid tin. Bluefish schools are marked by blood-tinged froth and squalling sea birds, and lone giants of the clan surprise anglers looking for other fish. No fish is a wilder adversary or more destructive of tackle.

An angler on a bluefish coast might have abundant good fishing, or hardly see bluefish at all, for the times of plenty and scarcity are measured in decades. Hal Lyman's chart of bluefish populations on the Massachusetts coast shows great numbers from before 1700 until 1764, when they disappeared in a slump that lasted until well after 1800. At mid-nineteenth century they reached a high peak, then faded again for no known reason. The fluctuations have continued.

THE SILVER KING

Until the tarpon was accepted as a new challenge, the striped bass had been the largest game fish regularly handled with rod and reel. Tarpon gave inshore fishermen a chance to use sporting tackle on an adversary that might weigh a hundred pounds or more. Fish were plentiful along the Florida coasts, especially in spring and summer; and Florida fishing for other species had been widely acclaimed before the Civil War.

For years there was little thought of using hook and line, and the tarpon was a good target for a spearman as it rolled or "blew" in island passes, one huge eye seemingly focused on boat and fisherman. Once the grain had been placed the fish was allowed to tow the boat to exhaustion. It was a fascinating target because of its polished silver appearance, its huge scales (much in demand by tourists), and its noisy, twisting jumps accompanied by clattering gill covers. It went by a variety of names: tarpum, silver king, *grand écaillé* (large scaled).

At first hook-and-line fishermen chose cumbersome shark tackle and found that the fish threw the bait or broke off almost instantly. Wondering if conventional gear could ever subdue the creature, writers filled fishing literature with suggestions for tackle, and one sportsman offered to pay the expenses for anyone who could catch a large specimen on rod and reel. Despite its seeming invincibility the tarpon was suited to light tackle properly employed. For one thing it spends much of its time in shallow water and deep sounding is a special curse of fragile equipment. Moreover, although tremendously powerful, the tarpon seldom runs for any distance at high speed and it can be followed in a boat. There also are ways of setting sharp hooks in tough tissue when they will not hold in the hard parts of the tarpon's jaw. Nonetheless, it was a new game for men who did not yet understand these things.

In 1885 William H. Wood caught a ninety-three-pound tarpon on rod and reel and the feat was widely acclaimed as a first by *Forest and Stream*. Immediately there were claims of earlier successes, but the important thing was that the rod and reel were beginning to work and "scientific anglers" had a chance with the great, big-eyed herring. If Wood had truly discovered a system, it was in letting the fish run unimpeded long enough to swallow the bait, or at least get it far enough into his gullet to give the hook a better chance.

Pilgrimages to Florida began in earnest. Giants were what they wanted and little attention was paid to the few anglers who used salmon rods and bright flies for smaller tarpon. By 1895 William C. Harris described the chosen tackle for tarpon in *The American Angler*. He recommended a good striped-bass reel with a leather guard sewed to one crossbar for thumb protection. It should hold five or six hundred feet of Cuttyhunk linen line and be attached to a short, stiff rod six to seven feet long. The hook should be a 10/0 O'Shaughnessy with three feet of soft linen or cotton snell "about the diameter of an ordinary lead pencil." H. C. Harmsworth, one of many English sportsmen to fish for tarpon in Florida, said he used a Vom Hofe reel called the "Silver King" and a seven-foot rod from Thomas J. Conroy, a leading tackle dealer.

~

The guide knows the cove well and when the tide will fill it. The bottom is firm sand and one end opens to an island pass which shows dark oyster-bar ridges at low tide and flows swiftly much of the time. As the incoming water slowly begins to build there are gentle eddies about the cove's narrow mouth, no more than seventy-five yards across. The barnacles clinging to mangrove roots crackle as they dry, and a hunting raccoon hurries along his tiny beach between water and higher ground, moving under a canopy of curved roots.

The bait is a foot-long mullet. The guide removes its head and uses a homemade tool to place the big hook so it protrudes slightly from the mullet's underside. He is careful not to let the bait touch the leader, for any slime will attract destructive crabs. He mutters when he sees a shark fin momentarily, but the shark turns back into the main channel. Carefully the guide reels the awkward bait to within a foot of the stiff rod tip and then casts it in a sweeping motion for perhaps a hundred feet. It is not exactly where he wants it; he tries again and is satisfied.

He takes twenty-five feet of line from the reel and coils it on a boat seat. On the last coil he lays a chip of wood to hold it. He pulls his ragged straw hat farther forward and slouches against the gunwhale to peer out at the cove's mouth. His client wonders whether he has gone to sleep. The light breeze, deadened by mangrove trees some seventy feet high, riffles the flat water only occasionally in small patches and the mosquitoes hum continually.

The tarpon come through the pass on the rising tide, rolling regularly and running downstream. Several of them enter the cove, examining the bottom four feet down. One pushes a swell along the shore and then tips to show most of its tail as it noses the sand for a crab. Another swell moves slowly in the direction of the bait and a big fish rolls sluggishly, its undershot jaw and staring eye plain to the watchers. The tarpon makes a sighing sound.

When the mullet is taken there is only a short movement of the coiled line under the chip, but then the line starts out steadily, the wisp of sound seeming loud to the tense fisherman. The fish stops to move off again, and then it goes into the air before the hook is set. It is suspended for an instant above a hole in the water and it crashes down in spray and foam.

The guide calls out happily, making the fish's name two words: "Tar-pon!" He accents the "pon," and the angler crowds the whirling spool, dry and hot under the leather guard. He remembers his instructions well and when the fish jumps again, higher than his head, he throws his weight on the rod to haul it down hard, its spine bent almost at right angles near the gills. He is gorge-fishing, although he has not used the word, and despite repeated jumps the tarpon is a dying fish. It will be pumped alongside the boat where the guide can strike it hard in the throat with his big gaff. Later there will be criticism of such still-fishing, but the method is followed today as it was nearly a hundred years ago and it is catching tarpon on rod and reel.

The tarpon became a craze for a time, and then Teddy Roosevelt charged up San Juan Hill, and across the continent, off Catalina Island, a man caught a bluefin tuna on a rod and reel.

5. A Gentled

Art

The fisherman stalked his quarry carefully. He had seen the trout rise from a considerable distance and he moved toward it from well downstream. At the tail of the pool he used his flies briefly, but he was thinking of the busy fish near the pool's head and watched for it as he worked the lower, slower current.

The pool was below a sharp bend of the river and water rushed into it from a rocky narrows, white and foamy over the shallow rocks and entering the big pool in a ridge of water that tapered away as it spread into the deeper section, leaving a train of large bubbles. At either side of the fast water the current curled and rolled, forming eddies and then slowing gradually in the depth of the pool's waist. The big trout was feeding near the fast water, unhurried and methodical, and as he rose his mouth made a plopping sound that carried to the fisherman over the river's mumbling, a sound that did not quite blend with the gurgles and hisses of the rapids.

The fisherman studied the contours of the pool: too many willows at the shore nearest the fish, too much depth in the center, and a low sun at the pool's head, certain to throw his shadow over the trout's lie if he approached from there. He knew it would be a long cast, and when he finally reached the place from which he had decided to make his attempt he was a little uncertain of the current. It pushed hard and piled a cushion of water against him.

He drew some line from his big reel and lifted his two flies in a movement that accelerated as it grew, the heavy line moving over his head like a living thing, flowing backward in a long loop that reflected the sun from its wet surface. He made one false cast a bit to one side and a tiny rainbow appeared for an instant in the delicate shower from his flies. He changed the direction of his cast slightly to put the flies directly over the fish, and as the rod tip came forward, hard bent with power, he released the hand-held line. It slithered through the guides, the cast straightening over the fish and the flies alighting slightly above it. They floated for a moment before the big trout took one of them in a business-like gulp. The rod tip came up briskly and bowed as the hook was set. Thousands of such trout have been hooked in hundreds of such pools.

THE ROD

The angler had made a truly long cast with a fly rod, using the weight of the line to carry his fly and leader, and he had fed more line as his cast went out. He was using a true rod with one hand and he had taught the rod to work for him. He could not say when or where he first did it. He had learned it gradually and his triumph was unannounced.

For five hundred years fishermen have improved rods, but it was well into the nineteenth century before they began to forecast the rod's full role. And as its importance expanded, thousands of designs and dozens of materials were applied.

For a long while nearly all of the best rods were made in combinations of various woods, often three kinds for a single shaft, sometimes more. No single cutting seemed to have appropriate stiffness in the butt, power in the middle section, and the essential flexibility at the tip. Perhaps natural cane rods came closest to the ideal.

Seasoned red cedar was a responsive material, but it broke easily and was considered satisfactory only for experts. Ash was widely used as butt material, often with middle and tip sections of lancewood. Greenheart from the West Indies and

South America was imported in large planks and cut to suit. There was mahoe from Cuba, hickory and ironwood from America, bethabara and snakewood from the Guianas, beefwood from Australia. Even Osage orange was tried, and Frank Forester recommended maple for butts. Whalebone was occasionally used for tips and Japanese workmen made some whalebone rods in the twentieth century. But all of these materials had serious defects, even though some of them would continue in use after split bamboo was developed.

Bamboo was used for rods and parts of rods long before it was "rent and glued," as the English described the laminating process. Calcutta cane came first, though eventually Tonkin cane was preferred. Some fishermen of the southern United States made rods of native cane, but it was not produced commercially. In 1975, the supply of Chinese cane being uncertain, manufacturers experimented with bamboo from other areas. The hand-built bamboo rod, almost forsaken by other fishermen, was returning as a favorite of trout anglers.

It is likely that the first split-bamboo rod sections were made in England, probably of three or four strips. Possibly the "rent and glue" process began because there were so many faulty pieces in shipments of imported bamboo.

Like many gunsmiths of his time, Samuel Phillippi of Easton, Pennsylvania, was a rodmaker (he also made violins). Between 1843 and 1845, he experimented with split bamboo, first making only rod tips with two, three, four, and six strips. He used ash for the butt sections at first, but in 1848 he sold his first all-bamboo rod in four strips. His son, Solon Phillippi, made his first six-section rod in 1859. Frank Forester wrote in 1855 that split bamboo in the proper quality was preferable to any other material.

Although the finest bamboo rods soon became the most desired, authorities repeatedly stated that cheap bamboo was inferior to other materials. Only a very small part of a shipment of bamboo could be used in rods. Sam Phillippi's bamboo spent almost a year reaching him from Asia, and almost anything could happen to the sticks on the way, including partial consumption by bugs.

In 1865 Charles F. Murphy of Newark, New Jersey, made the first split-bamboo salmon rod and then produced a split-bamboo bass rod. By 1870 H. L. Leonard began to market split bamboo, and that name survived on quality rods a century later. Charles Frederick Orvis, who had built rods since 1856, went to split bamboo in 1880.

Construction of nineteenth-century rods was complicated because the builders did not know what sort of action was needed. After the Civil War, angling took so many directions there was violent disagreement about bait rods, fly rods, trolling rods, and others of vague or all-around purpose. The "whippy" fly rod preferred by many in Britain had great influence at first, but when stiffer American rods began to get greater distance there was a search for rod "power" without the addition of too much weight, and nearly limitless ways of cutting and gluing bamboo developed.

Some rods were made round, and although that avoided the sharp corners that could be damaged in fishing mishaps it took away much of the bamboo needed for strength. Later the corners of six-sided rods were slightly rounded, but distinctly flat surfaces were left. Glue was the weakness of early split bamboo and extensive thread wrappings were used to support it, and to add stiffness. Some rods were solidly

98

*Theodore Gordon (above) appears as a
nattily dressed angler on the Neversink in 1912.
This is the only known photograph of
him while fishing. Angler below
employed jointed rod and huge creel, but location
of his fly reel suggests
occasional two-handed use. Right: Orvis prototype
reel is in foreground. Rods are
Phillippi (right) and early Leonard.*

TROUT FISHING.

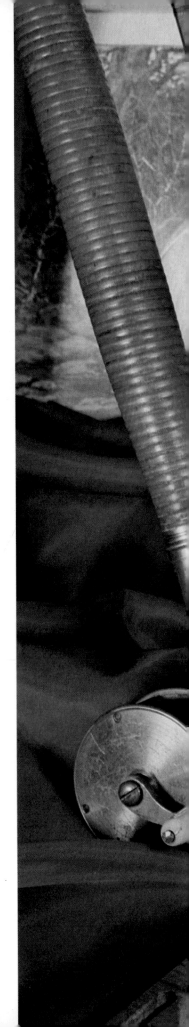

wrapped with thread, as were most buggy whips, and early makers had their individual designs. At one time extensive wrappings were a mark of better equipment.

Until World War I, calf glue was best for bamboo rods but it was never truly waterproof. Fishermen of later years who collected fine old rods and put them into their cases wet sometimes found only the thread wrappings holding them together the next time they were needed. After World War I, plastic resins solved the glue problem. For added strength some early builders went to double and even triple construction. In effect, that amounted to one rod inside another. Later there were hollow-built butt sections, a tube being stiffer for its weight than solid material. Impregnating bamboo for durability was undertaken by twentieth-century designers.

Steel reinforcement of bamboo was controversial. Some rods were ribbed with cross-hatched steel wire, others used steel as a core. While grave designers were photographed in dramatic demonstrations of the strength and stiffness of steel-and-bamboo combinations, prominent anglers talked of rod action and insisted that touching a rod tip to its butt had nothing to do with its fishing qualities.

Even the location of the reel on the rod handle was controversial. Of course, in casting bait the multiplying reel was ahead of the hand and on top of the rod, but in other kinds of fishing it might be located beneath the rod. Fly-fishermen were tending to reels below the hand and on the rod's underside but that transition was made slowly. Many of the multiplying reels for casting were also used on fly rods, and complex-appearing automatic fly reels were being made before the turn of the century.

Reels were fastened to rods with simple sliding rings, screws, or various seating devices. Some of the gleaming reel seats were in disfavor because they might frighten fish and were considered too garish by conservative sportsmen. "Presentation" rods were sometimes showy, with engraved plates in the reel seat section, and some were decorated by Tiffany, but ornamentation fell into disfavor and has never been popular since in the better rods.

Although fly casting was responsible for most early development of split-bamboo rods, some of the stand fishermen used them for striped bass and they were also used for trolling, often with alternate guides on opposite sides, so the strain of fishing could be equalized and a "set" avoided.

The old rod materials were persistent, and after 1900 there were lancewood rods available again, although the supply of wood from Cuba had been cut off temporarily during the Spanish-American War. Greenhart and bethabara never quite disappeared.

Advertising often was deceptive and some new names were invented for old materials. "Steel vine" rods, for example, were Calcutta bamboo. Gadgetry went with many of the early ones, hollow butt receptacles containing oil for use on metal ferrules or reels, and even scales for fish weighing.

Even when Americans managed to beat the British in angling endeavors the British sporting press was derogatory. In 1883 an international fisheries exhibition and casting tournament was held in London. A rod made by B. F. Nichols of Boston won the highest award for quality, and Reuben Wood, using a Nichols rod, won the casting tournament. Americans continued to win at competitive casting, but the British were unimpressed by either their skills or their equipment. Casting competition was popular in America long

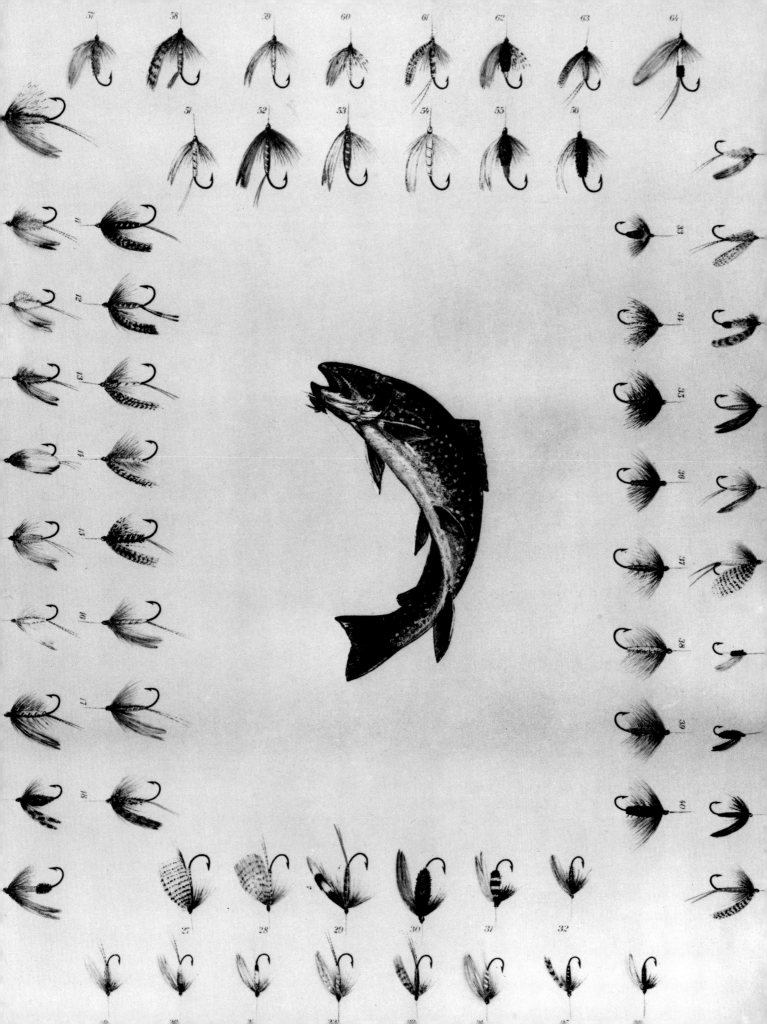

*Living mayfly (below) has been
inspiration for development of dry-fly angling.
Orvis calendar for 1900 advertises
pioneer American tackle concern. Early Orvis
flies are contrast to modern Royal
Coachman dry. Fly-tying vises of Theodore
Gordon (right) were tools of "father
of American dry-fly fishing" and appear in
collection of William Cushner.*

Currier & Ives were not the first to
poke fun at the fishing dandy, and fly anglers
were logical targets. Humorists find
the snagged fly irresistible, and living insects of
this fisherman's day were not confronted
by repellent. Detailed casting instruction from Frank
Forester (opposite) recommended use of
both hands, but did not show full body swing
of the modern surf-caster.

before the British trial of 1883. In 1864 Robert Roosevelt won a contest at a convention of New York sportsmen's clubs. By 1883 the fly-casting distances achieved were comparing well with those of modern fishermen, and in that year a competitor with a ten-foot rod of four and three-eighths ounces cast a fly eighty-five feet at a tournament in Central Park.

In fly-fishing Americans imitated and revered the English, but British fishermen often described American trout angling with fine scorn. In 1839 the *London Sporting Review* carried a report from an Englishman stating that American trout were too tame, that the country was too new for civilized fishing, and that he had repeatedly killed all of the trout counted in an American pool. That complainant reported he had speared muskellunge, evidently feeling they were not worthy of hook-and-line fishing. He had used long float lines for gray trout and had been annoyed by "filthy catfish."

THE NEW TROUT

In at least one respect the visiting British anglers were right: The brook trout was too easy to catch. It was also an easy victim of pollution and overheated waters, and extremely vulnerable to poachers.

The brilliant red and white fin of a brook trout tugged through the water or skittered across its surface would take other brook trout. The Parmachene Belle wet fly was an imitation of a fish's fin and effective enough, although no one knew why a trout should chase a duplicate of its own fin. The trout faded rapidly in the East. In 1838 an angler reported in the *Spirit of the Times* that Long Island trout were much larger than those found in New England, with fish of three or four pounds quite common, but by 1880 eastern trout fishing had suffered so badly that the editor of *Forest and Stream* proclaimed, "This is probably the last generation of trout fishers."

The brown trout turned the current. The trout of Walton, Cotton, and Dame Juliana came to America, a trout that had lived the history of Europe and Britain, and taxed the skills of the builders of fly-fishing.

There were introductions in the 1880s and at other times, some fish coming from Germany as the German Brown and others from Scotland

*Reels were seated variously on early
rods. Some were attached by sliding rings or
screws. Note that one on top
is simply tied on. Top: Bearded Frederic Halford,
beloved British angling writer,
and friends on a fishing expedition. Above:
Clear-running Pennsylvania streams
were prized by 19th-century anglers. One-handed
rod still had not made its appearance.*

as the Loch Leven, soon to mingle and be known simply as "brown trout." The brown was not to end its emigration in the United States, but was to cover the world. North American anglers later followed it to South America and to New Zealand. It was a special fish with unmatched qualifications. It could withstand warmer water than could the brook trout, it could live with civilization, and it refused flies the brookie seized with abandon. The brown trout came to stay.

The brown trout's habitat encompasses that of many other trout. In rainbow streams it often lies a little farther from the fastest water, glides through thickly weeded sloughs, and sometimes moves emergent plants gently as it forages against muddy banks. It has lived with the brookie, but tends to displace it and now patrols western runs alongside the cutthroat. It is found in hard-fished streams with rainbow trout, but if the fishing is too successful and the rainbows disappear the browns will remain.

And when man has done his worst to trout water—warmed, silted, and polluted it— and believes the trout are gone for good, some brown trout will stay until the last, probably heavy fish, unseen and unknown, but waiting for a change that may bring back cleaner water and usable spawning gravels. Often those things do happen and the clan multiplies again. In time the brown's very tenacity placed it in disfavor with fishermen, who learned that it often grows to great size while other species decline. The brown trout, they said, was a cannibal that destroyed the others. As with other trout, the large brown feeds upon small fishes and is a special hazard because its cunning makes it more likely to reach large size. Perhaps an overall stream population would be bettered if the largest brown trout were removed, but the known presence of unseen giants intrigues the fisherman, even if he catches only juveniles.

For the angler much of the brown's appeal is in its feeding habits, for large brown trout continue to take floating insects when other species of similar size have turned almost entirely to underwater forage. Producing and presenting an insect imitation for inspection by large and worldly fish is one of angling's great challenges.

Not only does the brown trout prefer insects at an age when other trout are pursuing minnows, but it often concentrates on insects which float. Anglers who first met the brown trout in America had to refine their approach to angling. Although nondescript wet-fly patterns required casting skills, as well as the study of water and current, the new fish made the successful fly-fisherman something of an entomologist. Wet flies, as they were generally fished, had imitated no living thing in action or appearance. When they were cast across current and allowed to swing downstream to be retrieved against the flow, they might follow the route of a minnow but they were not tied to imitate one. And if they were retrieved slowly in quiet lake water they might move like nymphs. Only when they drifted with the current did they resemble drowned insects in both form and lack of action. And, of course, for unlearned brook trout the niceties of insect form and behavior had been unnecessary. With the new brown trout they were not only helpful with both sunken and floating flies, but they added an appealing dimension which produced master trout anglers in America to match those of Great Britain.

For generations Old World fishermen had been writing of the intricacies of their art. Many American anglers had not related mayfly hatches to actual stream residence, believing that the flies simply lived and swarmed near water. But new kinds of fishing changed that. Master anglers have studied the mayflies of a single stream for a lifetime, and there have been meticulous tabulations of many eastern hatches. Almost a hundred years after "scientific" fly-fishing came with the brown trout, the myriad mayflies of most of the West were little understood and poorly cataloged. The first anglers to study the insects of eastern trout streams were to acquire belated fame among fishermen of another era. Most were less well-known in their lifetimes.

The mayfly's life begins typically as a nymph, a worm-like creature that drifts with the current, burrows in soft bottom, clings to stones or vegetation, or crawls beneath gravel and larger stones. Its life is a series of transformations or molts, and when it emerges as a fly it draws the attention of fishermen who have ignored it in the months or years it has been a part of an unseen underwater world. When a mayfly nymph floats to the surface and molts into a fly, it is then a *dun* or *subimago;* it dries its wings to leave the water, molts again, probably on nearby bushes, and returns to the stream to spawn as a *spinner* or *imago.* A mating dance of death ends with the deposit of eggs which will become nymphs and continue the cycle, while the mature flies die, sometimes drifting on backwaters in tiny windrows. The romance of the mayfly and its gauzy delicacy became a poetic theme of trout fishermen, who sought to imitate its various forms with artificial dry flies.

Hatches of the various insects can be predicted to some extent. At least they can be listed in the order of their emergence, if not by dates. Hatches vary from unobtrusive emergence of flies below shallow riffles to blizzards of large insects in whirling patterns over large rivers.

As anglers learned about insects, they learned the ways trout consumed them, the matters of feeding stations, and how individual fishes rise in a repeated pattern, returning to their chosen lies after each venture. In England, where such things were already orderly, there were fishermen who only "fished the rise," uninterested in seeking fish which had not revealed themselves by surface disturbance. They learned to read not only the hatch, if it were visible, but also the rise forms of the trout, and learned to tell the splash of the darting fingerling from the dimple, swirl, or plop of worthwhile trout.

As brook trout declined in the East and brown trout arrived, it was the time and place for Theodore Gordon and the dry fly. The very first mention of such flies was in George Scotcher's *The Fly Fisher's Legacy,* published in England in 1800, and the surface fly turned up again in George P. R. Pulman's *Vade Mecum of Fly Fishing for Trout* in 1841, although these flies were not the high floaters of later years, apparently being ordinary wet flies that floated briefly when properly cast. The dry fly produced codes, cults, and some snobbery, but it was most important as an encouragement of truly "scientific fishing." That term had long been used to describe studious and sportsmanlike conduct.

THE GORDON SCHOOL

The personal life of Theodore Gordon is an important part of fishing history, for it explains his contribution. He was born to a prosperous family in Pittsburgh in 1854. As a youth he fished the limestone streams of Pennsylvania, thus beginning in some of the most "scientific" water of America, though the brown trout was

not yet present. He remained a bachelor and retired as a young man to a haven on the Neversink in the New York Catskills. He was slight of build and in ill health for much of his life, evidently suffering from tuberculosis. He died in 1915 after devoting his life to the trout stream as a semirecluse. He had fished in southern waters, but it was his concentration on the eastern streams and their insects that brought him belated fame. John McDonald, author and fishing historian, was a leader in the later study of his life, and when he and other researchers located Gordon's grave there was no indication of the man's contributions to angling.

Gordon was a student of fishing literature, both American and English, and he had employed the same sort of pseudo-dry-fly fishing described by Thad Norris, using wet flies but drying them

in false casting. He was an "upstream fisherman" before he learned of the dry fly and its English origin. The upstream cast allowed the fly to drift "dead" with the current, the perfect presentation showing no trace of leader tug—truly "scientific" fishing.

The origin of the British dry fly is vague, but Frederic Halford was its English advocate. In 1890 Gordon wrote a letter of inquiry to him and received a set of Halford's drys. Halford's were imitations of British insects, but from them Gordon developed ties for his own water. He was more than an imitator, however, for the American streams were swifter, and a creation that floated well on a placid chalk stream might have a short career on bouncing rapids, so Gordon tied flies with stiff hackles to make them more buoyant than British flies. Good dry-fly hackles have

Old salmon fly from William Cushner collection shows complex color details and careful workmanship. Right: Salmon angler casts in early morning fog on Miramichi River in New Brunswick. Fish are known to be in deeper water near opposite shore. S.A. Kilbourne's painting, "Caught," showing brookie on wet fly, is probably best-known trout picture of all time.

the property of holding the fly's body and most of the hook away from the water, and showing the rising fish a cluster of indentations on the surface film, much like those impressed by an insect's legs. And Gordon went on from there, a reclusive figure on his beloved pools, never rigidly addicted to any cult, but employing both wet and dry flies as conditions demanded. Professional fly tiers of his time were taught some of his devices and those teachings were fondly followed long afterward.

There is only one photograph of Gordon on the stream: a nattily attired little fisherman accompanied by a lady angler, probably the one he complimented anonymously in print when he described her energy and fishing enthusiasm. Gordon wrote "Little Talks On Fly Fishing" in *Forest and Stream* and, beginning in 1890, was American correspondent for England's *Fishing Gazette*. Some of his best writing, however, was in his correspondence with leading fishermen of his time. The Quill Gordon, still a popular fly, was his creation, but he dressed it in different ways to fit different situations.

There have been many other Americans who for one reason or another left all other pursuits and devoted their lives to sport fishing, but Gordon was unique because he lived at the beginning of classic fly-fishing in America, and perhaps he deserves his title as its father, at least where trout are concerned. Through him, British angling traditions were renewed in America; and the brown trout had arrived. But before the Americans went their separate ways, there were still a few English matters to be reckoned with.

The classic dry fly in England

SALMON FISHING.

dated from midcentury, but when Halford wrote of it in the eighties, and his associates adopted it as the end-all of trout fishing, the wet fly became a second-class citizen when fished upstream and something worse when fished downstream. The English, swathed in the ethics of sport, took a wet-fly/dry-fly controversy very seriously. A dry-fly fisherman going upstream was disturbed to meet a wet-fly fisherman coming down, especially if he was using a cast of three or four flies. There were certain things one did not do on certain streams, and there were some anglers who felt it was unethical to "fish the water" when no fish were seen rising. Such niceties were lost on Americans at that time.

Later, John Waller Hills wrote of the "intolerant dictatorship" of the dry fly. When G. E. M. Skues came forth with his *Minor Tactics of the Chalk Stream* in 1910, he favored nymphs or wet flies for certain conditions and used nymphs on rising fish. Then there was a long feud between dry-fly fishermen and nymph fishermen in England, the nymph gaining stature when it proved—often—to require more skill than the dry fly. At any rate, while the English civil war of method raged on, Americans, following Gordon, finally turned away from British prejudices, fished both wet and dry, and never again were influenced more than casually by the British, except in regard to equipment.

Edward Ringwood Hewitt (1866-1957) fostered the popularity of the nymph on American waters, designed his own, and was one of the early practitioners of dry-fly fishing for salmon. Born to great wealth, he grew up in New Jersey and was a student of fish and fish culture as well as angling techniques, fishing for salmon and trout over much of the world and writing perceptive accounts of his findings.

All early salmon rods—this one is 1855—
were two-handed weapons, usually of great length
and frequently with a sharp butt that
could be stuck into ground while angler rested
his arms. Lighter salmon rods
were used in America long before British accepted
them. Many English fishermen still
use two-handers. Uselessly tiny gaff hook
may have been artist's error.

His "skaters" were effective dry flies, and he gained fame as a user of ultralight tackle on Atlantic salmon, a pursuit in which he was followed by Lee Wulff, himself an originator of flies, especially highly visible hair-winged patterns. Hewitt and his fishing companion, George LaBranche, had great influence on studious fishermen of the nineteen-twenties and later.

THE FLIES

Named flies have run to the thousands, most of their origins obscured, but their names have often established their popularity, especially in the case of gaudy specimens resembling no particular insect. The best-known fly in America is the Royal Coachman, said to have been named by L. C. Orvis, who added the "Royal" when he studied a colorful variation of the Coachman, a fly that originated in England. The original Coachman is credited to a real coachman-fisherman named Tom Bosworth, who served the royal family—George IV, William IV, and Queen Victoria. The Parmachene Belle was named after Parmachene Lake in Maine before 1900.

At one time, Charles Orvis had proposed the logical but unromantic plan of giving flies numbers instead of names, and had such a system been followed it is doubtful if many of the favorites of today would have survived. It is difficult to forget names like Thunder and Lightning, Goofus Bug, Yellow Sally, and Rat-faced MacDougall.

In imitating some five hundred mayflies with fur and feathers the tiers have brushed close to nature, and many a fisherman has squinted his smarting eyes to tell his artificial from a parade of naturals sliding down a trout stream. And thousands of times fishermen have set their hooks against nothing as trout have gulped living flies floating close to counterfeit wisps of feather and steel.

Tradition moved in mysterious ways with Atlantic salmon flies. For the most noble fish of all, anglers preferred ties of beauty, and salmon fishermen have generally been a bit on the aristocratic side, able to afford attractions of careful workmanship and exotic materials. As a result, a traditional salmon fly might cost several times the price of a trout fly; its feathers are "married" or interwoven, and a box of them may be displayed with the same reverence applied to custom rods or firearms. American salmon fishers still cling to tradition to some extent, but some tiers in a hurry have demonstrated that simple and inexpensive salmon flies can be just as effective as those of exotic birth.

Dry-fly fishing for Atlantic salmon came long after the dry was first used for trout, and salmon drys have tended toward the bushy designs used for unprincipled rainbow trout of big western rivers, even though the very first were modifications of wet patterns.

THE RAINBOW

Until after the Civil War, sportsmen had accepted fish populations much as they came. They had complained that the brook trout were fading, and when the salmon "moved north" they read regretfully of times past, when a man could stand with feet apart in shallow water and kill a barrel of Atlantic salmon with an ax as they passed between his knees, but they did little transplanting except for the black bass.

Western trout were little understood until late in the century. The rainbow was known as the "mountain trout," or "California trout," but most

Traditional equipment of classical
fly-fisherman is shown in painting by George Cope.
Soft hat, pipe, and flask are part of
popular "uniform," as is wicker creel. Reel is
mounted below the hand, but cork
handle was not yet popular. Many rod shafts
were of solid wood until 1900 and
solid materials were not entirely replaced by
split bamboo long after that.

sports fishermen did their traveling in the eastern part of the country.

The rainbow is the hardest-fighting trout and lives in the fastest water. To the first sportfishermen who caught them it must have appeared the fish survived in the crashing white water itself, for its lie is often roofed by cascades and spray. But the fish finds shelter even in those places. On the bottom are little depressions and hidden rocks that create small patches of slowed current where it holds with little effort, darting upward at its hurtling food. Where large boulders break the surface the rainbow waits on the very edge of the divided torrent, and where the boulder slows upstream water into a bulging cushion the rainbow often holds above the obstruction instead of below it. An angler experienced with other trouts who has tried to drift his fly past the boulder is suprised to find it taken before it reaches the logical place.

The rainbow is native from the high mountains of northern Mexico to the Aleutian Islands, and a fish of eastern Russia evidently is a very close relative. The rainbow appeared in so many colors that early fishermen thought they were dealing with a dozen kinds of trout instead of one. In some clear lakes the fish lacks spots, and in some streams it has a brilliant red side, possibly with bold black spots. As a parr its color is different still, and the first violent silver fish that appeared in Pacific salmon nets with a metallic sheen to its head was simply called a salmon trout. It was, of course, the steelhead, which fishermen thought was yet another fish.

Although there is habitat where the brown trout may outlast the rainbow, the latter can withstand higher temperatures for short periods, surviving for some time even at eighty degrees. Like the brown trout it has covered much of the globe as a transplant.

The rainbow, whether anadromous or a fresh-water resident, spawns from January through the spring in most waters, although spawning may occur in later summer in high country. Spawning is in redds similar to those of salmon, but the rainbow does not die afterward, like the Pacific salmon, and is more likely to survive several spawnings than the Atlantic salmon. All trouts have strains that go to sea, but it is believed the others have more restricted ranges in salt water, while the steelhead races the salmon and is known to have traveled more than two thousand miles on its spawning migration. There is no visible difference between the young rainbow that will spend its life in fresh water and the one that will range the ocean, but the migrating urge is inherited. The rainbow's migratory habits are less rigid than the salmon's.

Fresh from ocean travels the steelhead returns in contingents or as single fish, possibly to spend considerable time in fertile brackish estuaries before the river journey.

The steelhead, unlike the salmon, feeds after it enters the rivers. The trip duplicates that of the salmon at first, the sea silver darkening, and the fish tiring and weakening as it breasts the current and the oft-recounted obstacles. As it nears its destination it may take the lure of a fisherman who will think he has hooked a spent salmon and when he has landed it he may wonder how a steelhead could be so sluggish. But if the fish has come early to the river it may change once more before it spawns. It will become even darker, and the band along its side may turn blood-red as vigor returns and weight is regained. Now the fisherman finds a very different fish, one with the weight of ocean

feeding and the agility of a resident rainbow.

In some rivers the steelhead will be small, less than ten pounds, but there are other strains of fish that will grow to forty. The size is not keyed to the stature of the native river and each watershed has its own strains, large or small. In some rivers there are large runs of summer steelhead months ahead of their spawning schedule, fish that rise to surface insects and are caught on dry flies.

There are fresh-water steelhead of large lakes that find tributary streams for their spawning, and sometimes the distinction between steelhead and resident rainbow is questionable. There are rainbows of small brooks that never see broader water and there are rainbows of small lakes. All of this was confusing to discoverers of rainbow trout before the fish had a name, but when the species had been partly identified its patrons recognized its hardiness and it was moved east to rivers and lakes where the brookie had faltered. In many places in the West it lived with brown trout, cutthroats, or brook trout, and even with grayling. In proper places it became a steelhead; or were those introduced steelhead to begin with? After a hundred and fifty years biologists were not quite sure, but they found they could develop strains that thrived in hatchery tanks and ponds.

Introduction of rainbow and brown trout was not always with the approval of resident fishermen. Especially in New England, some regarded the new fish as interlopers. The brown trout was not so good to eat as the brookie, they said. Later there were arguments about the relative merits of the brown and the rainbow. Some master fishermen preferred the resourceful brown, while the occasional fisherman found the rainbow easier to catch. It developed that the rainbow was easiest of all to raise in captivity and capable of withstanding rough handling.

Trout of some of America's most remote wilderness are a paradox. While man destroyed habitat in the lowlands he carried fish to high lakes and creeks that no trout could have reached unaided, waters that had been sealed off in formation of the mountains.

SALMO SALAR

When the Atlantic salmon withdrew from the southerly portions of its range, it was followed by those who had called it the king of game fish and its greater distance from their homes added to its attraction. In crowded thousands it had been only a harvestable commodity, in lesser numbers it had become a valued sport fish, and with scarcity and remoteness it became an angling prize.

The salmon often moved in modest streams, but sometimes leaped in a frame of spray and sometimes ascended torrents like a magnified trout. It was trout fishermen who treasured the salmon and it has been a fly fish for almost as long as the brown. Much of the salmon's appeal is in the quieter pools, where a twenty-pound fish may stir a silent swirl for an unknown reason and then retire to a chosen lie, finning in moving water that must move just so. For a long time the fish may stay there, its fins weaving just enough to hold it against the current, swimming as if preoccupied with the more important task to come.

Salmon fishermen need no knowledge of the natural insects of their rivers, for the fish are not supposed to feed on their return from the sea. The very fact that the salmon takes a fly at all is a contradiction and adds to the sport's appeal. And since they had no reason to imitate real insects the tiers of salmon flies formed their creations with imagination, producing exotic things that became traditional and employed feathers from the corners of the world. Their names were sometimes descriptive of the colors used, sometimes honored famous fishermen, and sometimes merely began with a smile at a tier's bench.

Even though the flies did not imitate any living insect there were definite preferences in the various rivers, both as to size and pattern. There were large, heavily dressed flies for high and cloudy water, and skimpily adorned hooks for low, clear water. Salmon fishermen found different tactics necessary in different waters, but the most common approach was with a fly swinging across the current above the fish's nose, just under the surface, usually cast across and downstream. No salmon fishermen knew just what such a fly represented, for no minnow or insect followed such a route, but the salmon demanded that the fly should come just so and expert anglers learned to present it that way.

There were some anglers on some waters who found their success improved when they "mended," or threw little curves in their casts, so that the fly swung broadside before the fish. They explained that with the usual method the fish saw the swinging fly only from the rear and could tell nothing of its form. In some rivers the broadside presentation was highly successful, but in others the salmon preferred the simple swing of the fly across its path and often was particular as to just how it swung, even if the fish saw little of it broadside.

Then there was the ruse of rigging the fly so that it swung on top of the water and created a gentle wake, and the salmon angler learned that he must change flies when a fish refused to take.

Thus he changed from one indefinite something to another indefinite something to take a fish, or he might change back to the original and take a fish, making salmon fishing an intriguing mixture of precise skills and pseudoscience.

There were guesses that the salmon took flies from memory of its former life as a darting parr in the same waters. Perhaps returning to the river took the fish back to its youth and caused it to strike tiny bits of feather after years of deep running in the open ocean where it fed on larger things. Eventually, the salmon fishermen found they could use floating flies successfully at times, flies that simply drifted with the current without action of their own, and this complicated the puzzle more than ever.

But the salmon stood out as a game fish because it took very small objects fished with a fly rod, so it was natural that tackle would become lighter. Despite the salmon's gleaming leaps and hissing runs, it was generally in fairly shallow water and could not sulk on a deep bottom. Then, too, it was somewhat confined in most cases by the limits of a pool, and it had none of the native trout's tendency to hide in underwater cover. It was an open-water fish.

The very long and heavy salmon rod gave way in America—a break with British tradition—to rods of weight and length suitable for bass or large trout. While the British continued with their two-handed rods both in Canada and in the home islands, the Americans went lighter and lighter, sometimes to an extreme.

The salmon runs dwindled in New England, and sportsmen traveled farther and farther, making the salmon an aristocratic quarry by its very cost and scarcity, as well as by its nature.

6. The Waters

Change

Only river sounds and the voices of passengers accompanied the early Ozark johnboats on their lazy trips down the bass rivers of Missouri and Arkansas. They left the little mountain towns and the railway stations to slide between the lazy hills for days, or even weeks. Many of the fishermen who rode them came from cities a long way off. They treasured their escape from formal society and from the complex worries of a growing industrial nation. Anyone busy with his tackle for the first few minutes of the float would have been surprised, looking back, to find the little landing out of sight and the hill country solitude already closing in.

It was two fishermen and one guide to a boat, the guide steering through fast water with his home-made paddle and working in measured thrusts in the slow pools. The guide was a mountain man in a mountain man's garb. In summer his hat was straw and in fall it might be black felt, and at all times he wore bib overalls. He sat on his spare clothing which was done up in a burlap bag.

In summer the hills were green, in fall, red and gold. There were miles of traveling with no sign of human life on shore, and then there might be the rocky clearing of a hill farm on the shoulder of one of the slopes, and the guide might stare silently at it as though expecting to sight an acquaintance.

The smallmouth bass came from the foot of the rocky bluffs, from the sucking eddies below the swift shoals, from the willow strands, and sometimes from the chunk rock in the deep, slow pools. They came in bronze streaks, often turning away from the plugs or flies and darting under the boats. When they struck they sometimes jumped wildly, and some-times the fisherman could see the hooked fish well down in the clear water, gyrating violently as it fought the lure. The lures had well-known names, some of which have survived, together with the lures themselves. Others have been long forgotten.

On some days there were quiet sloughs off the main river, and in that slower water there might be largemouth bass—"linesides," the guides called them. Now and then there would be green sunfish or rock bass, if the lures were small enough.

For small parties each boat carried its own supplies, its food and wall tent and cooking utensils, and the guide served as camp cook. For large parties there was a commissary boat that went ahead to each night's camping spot, generally on a gravel bar. When the fishermen arrived, camp would be set up and supper cooking.

Late evening in the hill country was a special time. The cool river canyon carried the scent of wood smoke and the inevitable hound sang from a distant ridge. A zealous guide might set a trout line for channel catfish, saying he never could abide bass to eat, and the wanderers would sleep to the river's song. Breakfast came with mist on the river. The camp was reduced to bundles and boxes, and reloaded onto the red plank boats, about twenty feet long. Under way the fishermen sat on folding chairs; they could see gray squirrels scampering in the shoreline trees, or occasionally, as the boat rounded a bend, a whitetail deer, and ducks taking off noisily from the backwaters. Some of them nest in Ozark country.

When the days or weeks ended, the boats grated ashore at a landing scarred by their predecessors and were loaded aboard wagons for the short trip to a railroad station surrounded by a cluster

*Opening pages: Rainbow trout became
America's favorite, spreading its range from western
slopes to replace less hardy species
across the continent. It could withstand more
pollution and higher temperatures than
the brookie and grayling. Early sports fishermen
(below) used heavy rods and relied
on native guides to open wilderness waters
for Canadian salmon fishing.*

*"Flooded deserts" (left) were result
of power dams in the West. These anglers use
modern inflated boat and outboard
motor to fish Lake Powell in Arizona and Utah.
Impoundment bass fishing (below) often takes place
around partly submerged trees.
Dams provide unique fishing below spillways
where water may be cold. Winslow Homer's largemouth
bass is an impoundment standby.*

*Sporting art of the 19th century
stressed fishes similar to those which had
been followed by Europeans. Pike,
Atlantic salmon, and American brook trout are
prominent in this painting by
E.F. Palmer in 1866. Artists of the day were
less careful in details
of panfish, and the black bass was not yet
recognized as the leading quarry.*

of cabins and a false-fronted store or two. The guides went back to their starting place to prepare the boats for another trip. The anglers left for home.

The float trip was never unique to the Ozark country. In various forms it appeared in many parts of the South and in the far northern wilderness, where the boat was generally a canoe and the drifters were more likely to surprise moose than raccoons. But the Ozark float had some of the elements of all such trips and perhaps it was better organized than the others; certainly it was very popular. It did not have the tense adventure of a rubber raft down a western cascade, and it did not penetrate the wilderness like a canoe on the Canadian border, but it was symbolic of man's escape by inland waterways. The Ozark float trip lost out largely to the demand for water power and is now merely a bit of angling nostalgia for those who watched the changes coming forty years ago.

The dams came slowly at first. Only an occasional one was needed to provide the modest amounts of electricity needed. But when building began to boom they soon curbed most of the larger float rivers and the changes they wrought in the fisheries were immediate and extreme. In a sense, the waters were lost to the wilderness fisherman and became those of the vacationing family. A way of fishing was gone forever. The new lakes were for new generations.

When the dam stills the river, the fertile bottomlands are covered and produce a wealth of food for thousands of fast-growing bass and panfish, more than the river ever supported. While the waters still are rising the fisherman may cast among flooded green trees, whether in the Ozarks or in California, and find the bass there. New impoundments have some of the best fishing of all, but they are keyed to a rigid schedule. After the new fish of the lake reach their maximum number and size, they suffer from the inexorable aging of all impoundments and the fishing recedes from its early peak. In other lakes the waters are unable to support large fish populations, and water skiing and boating take the place of angling. Below the dam, where the river continues to follow its old course, there are changes, too. The water emerging from some of the larger spillways is so much colder than before that trout have taken the place of the bass.

So the smallmouth bass stream is frequently a casualty of the impoundment, as is the free-flowing trout stream. In other cases the impoundment affords fishing water where there was little or none before. In the arid West a fisherman catches bass among freshly drowned cactus plants, or at the mouths of formerly inaccessible cliff caverns.

For the most part the trout and salmon streams are colder than smallmouth waters and run faster. Float-fishing came to them somewhat later simply because they tended to be located in more remote sections where the boating was difficult. High-bowed skiffs, held against the current by oars, allowed the anglers to slow their descent on wild rivers. They could fish from the boat itself or could stop at likely spots and wade or fish from the bank. The McKenzie boat, a craft designed much like the salt-water dory, has in late years been a mainstay for the floater of swift trout and steelhead rivers. The boat comes down bow first but the stern sits high and the oarsman can slow his progress and use the current for steerage.

The inflatable boat came into its own after World War II, first as an unwieldy life raft and then as a craft designed for steering in swift water. It is among the safest of fast-water boats, although less

*Brown trout imported from Europe
showed ability to reach great size in streams
where even the rainbow failed,
and required advanced methods that had not been
necessary for the easier brook trout.
High-mountain trout became targets of pack
expeditions, and fish were taken to
lakes that had been barren before. High lakes
were a last frontier for anglers.*

*Fishes of the Rocky Mountain area were
hardly known by American sportsmen until after
eastern salmon streams began to
give out. Sport fishing was of little interest to
earliest settlers, but by 1880 anglers
were taking long trips purely for sport. Rainbow and
cutthroat trout, grayling and
Rocky Mountain whitefish became known to
easterners seeking new horizons.*

manageable in most designs. Later inflatable boats were shaped like outboard skiffs and often used motors. Canoes and kayaks, the craft of many white-water anglers, operate on a different principle from that of most float boats. They depend on forward momentum for steerage and must travel faster than the current, whereas the float boat is held back against it. Thus it is used as a place-to-place conveyance on fast water and little fishing is done from it there.

While the damming of bass rivers could produce great lakes with room for more fish and fishermen, the damming of trout and salmon rivers usually degraded the fishing and sometimes stopped it altogether. Much of the charm of trout and salmon fishing is in running water and the task of interpreting it. Lake fish perform differently, generally demanding coarser methods. The twentieth-century fly-fisherman bitterly watched roaring rivers altered to sluggish lakes where he had to troll deep with outlandish lures in order to catch fish. And there were other, more ominous developments.

The Pacific salmon began to disappear early from the southernmost part of their range. Their rivers of migration suffered from estuary pollution and from upstream dams. The twentieth-century Columbia River changed from a roaring watercourse to a chain of enormous impoundments, and the problem of getting migratory salmon over dams and through polluted areas was never entirely solved. Federal and state fish hatcheries have come to the partial rescue of many salmon runs, producing fingerlings that will return to their original waters to spawn, an artificial production of fish that may visit the shores of Japan and still come home when their travels are done.

A dam that cut off migrating fish and made a lake of a river was easily understood, but civilization brought other developments that were more subtle. In the East, in a gradual deterioration that began with the Pilgrims, lumbering and farming destroyed the salmon rivers. The same practices decreased populations of trout and anadromous shad.

A naturally forested riverbank throws enough shadow to help cool the water in hot weather. Hardwoods which shed their leaves admit sun in winter when it is needed. Once the trees are cut there is no protection from sun, and a sudden thaw after heavy snowfalls can cause destructive floods. With native trees gone, erosion frequently follows heavy rain or snow, filling streams with silt. This process may be hastened if agriculture also has removed shrubs and grasses that held the soil.

A beaver pond that provided a deep retreat for brook trout in normal periods of cold or heat can be filled with silt until it has contrary effects, becoming very shallow and spreading the stream's water until it is over-quickly warmed or frozen. The erosion of stream banks causes the bed to widen and become shallow and similarly vulnerable to extremes of heat and cold. The silt washing from crumbling banks will cover gravelly or stony bottoms, destroying the habitat of insect life and ruining spawning areas, for it is the rocky stretches that are most stable and essential for the welfare of trout.

Log drives down the eastern waterways had their own devastating effects. They jammed and wrecked natural banks, while the bark from thousands of tons of timber turned to sludge on the river bottoms. But these effects were gradual and attracted less attention than heavy commercial fishing.

The disposal of waste material

from cities and factories began as an innocent and logical process, although once it had become routine practice the trend was hard to alter without great expense. The sins of the pioneers were multiplied in twentieth-century pollution.

While nineteenth-century writers bewailed the effect of steamboat traffic, plans to make navigation simpler rushed forward. Channelization was one answer to shipping problems, and dredges huffed away, deepening and straightening riverbeds. With the channels accomplished, the flood waters came through in a rush. The vegetation that supported so much underwater life vanished and drought followed flood. While the West became involved with power dams that slowed the swift rivers, the South suffered from channelization that speeded slow ones. Meandering courses that had moved through reeds and grasses were changed into arrow-straight ditches that accepted swift boat traffic, but lost the purification process that had accompanied the meanders. The fish that had thrived in networks of lazily flowing, vegetated channels became scarce in canals.

In upland trout country, small streams were crowded by implacable rivals—the highway and the railroad. The streams followed valleys or canyons which also were the logical places for rails and wagon roads, and later for superhighways. The builders did not destroy the creeks and rivers but they diverted them and coated their stones and gravels with silt. The aquatic insect life destroyed by such construction has been enormous and the destruction still goes on. But, of course, in the beginning hardly anyone was aware of the delicate balances within a trout stream.

If the roads and railroads had first priority, irrigation needs were truly sacred. Simple ditching and flumes could divert water from a mountain stream and take it miles away from the riverbed, allowing downstream sections to stagnate and dry up. Water rights are legal complexities and tons of fish have died in irrigation ditches.

Estuaries of brackish water have neither the timbered beauty of mountain streams nor the blue of deep water, and they often have been considered an obstacle to shipping as well as to harbor construction, so many of our port cities stand where marshes and swamps once met the sea. But "marsh" and "swamp" were terms for wasteland in those days, and as the twentieth century draws to a close their true value is finally being realized. Brackish water is the incubator of the sea and no fresh or truly salt water carries the swarms of life that fill brackish inlets. This was not known when the cities grew above the marshes and it probably would have made no difference if it had, for the myth of the endless supply is always hard to destroy.

Conservationists of the nineteenth century and early twentieth century worried little about habitat, for they reasoned that water, if reasonably pure, was water, and they were sure that fresh-water fish destroyed by malpractice could be restored by planting. The ocean, they assumed, could take care of itself, for only the edges had been fished and any lack of salt-water fish would be temporary.

The introduction of native fish to new waters continued and it is likely that black bass were "started" innumerable times in waters where they had already taken hold. The western trouts were carried from creek to creek in buckets and coffeepots. There were stories of trout optimistically being introduced to the waters of midwestern ponds in mid-summer!

*"Float fishing" takes sportsmen away
from crowded streams. The McKenzie boat with high
bow and stern is built for very swift
mountain rivers with oarsman steering from stern.
Canoe requires great skill in white
water. Johnboat (with motor) is Ozark standby.
Inflated boat can be taken to high
country and rough water. Lamprey (bottom) changed
Great Lakes fishing picture.*

The brown and rainbow trouts were perpetually introduced and in nearly every new home they were welcome, although some residents of Maine felt that "foreign" trout, like bass, were not needed. By the twentieth century, fish managers had learned that in most cases there is no turning back once fish have been introduced.

Most successful plantings are well worthwhile. The striped-bass fingerlings were taken from the East Coast to the Sacramento River delta in 1886. First the energetic fish populated the San Francisco Bay area, and then multiplied as far south as Los Angeles and as far north as Washington state. It became a leading sport fish of the coast and is caught on sporting tackle in bays, rivers, and surf.

The American shad, taken to California from Rochester, New York, by the noted fish culturist Seth Green, accepted its new home and prospered. And it was Green who brought the rainbow eastward.

But European carp became an American folly. At a time when anglers were still arguing as to what was a game fish and what was not, the carp got a foothold which is unlikely ever to be relinquished. It was introduced in the misguidedly enthusiastic spirit that also brought the English sparrow and the starling, and like them it has stayed to become a national liability.

There are places where carp are desirable, and they are satisfactory food fish when properly prepared, but they are persistent enemies of game fish. Their hallowed place in the Orient must have influenced the Americans who used them as a sort of political commodity while fishing authorities pleaded for caution. In Europe, where carp seemed to mesh harmlessly with more aristocratic residents, carp fishing is a highly regarded sport.

Carp are capable of withstanding extremes of temperature and can remain dormant in very cold weather, their durability making them excellent subjects for transport and fish farming. There are stories of private carp ponds and broken dams at earlier dates, but the carp officially arrived in the eighteen-seventies as guests of the United States Fish Commission, accompanied by glowing accounts from abroad. They multiplied so willingly in Baltimore ponds that it was soon possible for congressmen to parcel them out to receptive constituents, and their desirability was enhanced by promotional publicity.

It took some time for the carp to reveal its destructive tendency toward the bottoms of game-fish lakes and rivers. Through rickety dams and careful plantings the big-scaled saboteur joined trout, bass, and pike in prime water all over the nation. The carp grubbed on the bottom, destroyed vegetation needed by native species, and spread thousands of acres of choking mud. Its endless millions of eggs hatched and flourished, and futile attempts to curb the fish's spread began while enthusiastic proponents continued to haul more carp to new communities.

Anglers encountering carp for the first time mistook their nuptial leapings for those of bass, and rowed eagerly toward these shallow-water splashings, only to meet spreading clouds of mud where violent carp spawning exercises were under way. Spawning carp create acres of churning water. (Although there are some times when carp can be taken on artificials, and even on surface lures, they are more often caught on flavored doughballs.)

Once the carp was established,

conservationists began to plot its eradication, but nothing worked. Spear and bow-fishing were encouraged, but the carp was here to stay, largely at the expense of more valued species. It was the one deliberate large-scale introduction that backfired. A hundred years later there was controversy over a special kind of carp, the huge white amur or grass carp from Russia, which was being selectively introduced to reduce excessive vegetation in waters of the United States.

Like the canaries of years ago which warned coal miners of bad air, the Michigan grayling was an early indicator of deterioration. It demands even more ideal conditions than the brook trout and was wiped out by the nineteen-thirties. The first fishermen to cast flies in Michigan found the grayling thick. Then they found brook trout taking over, and before 1900 they reported the grayling doomed. The Manistee and Au Sable rivers, famous trout streams, had held large populations of grayling at one time, but the areas were easily reached by railway and grayling angling was well advertised as a novelty for eastern sportsmen. There were reports of hundreds of fish caught in a single day. Commercial fishing also was wasteful and insistent, and streamside lumbering was quickly destructive of grayling habitat.

The Montana grayling is nearly identical to the Michigan fish and maintains a precarious foothold in the high West, although the best grayling fishing is now in Canada and Alaska. Besides the remoteness of its habitat, it is protected by its size, for it is not large enough to be exciting on any but the lightest tackle and in most grayling waters a fish of ten inches is a large one. The Northwest Territories have reported the largest grayling. In Great Slave Lake they are known to have reached five pounds. Its fascination is in the delicacy of its feeding habits, the beauty of the wild country in which it is found, and its subtle form and colors.

So sensitive is the grayling to habitat changes that its introduction has been sketchy, and many plantings that seemed highly successful for a time have simply disappeared, not always for discernible reasons. The high lakes where they have been placed have sometimes supported populations which flourished briefly, but faded within a season.

Although not as selective as trout, the grayling can tantalize the fisherman with repeated rises and refusals. Sometimes they seem to prefer the sort of presentation that will drive trout away, and it is not unusual for grayling to take dragging dry flies in brisk current when they have refused what seem to be perfect drifts.

The caster locates a pod of grayling by their feeding dimples and casts his small fly just above them. There are little splashes and urgent swirls about his offerings, and he strikes repeatedly but hooks nothing. It is likely the fish are simply chasing his fly and when he changes its size or color he may have immediate strikes. Most fly-fishermen think of grayling as small-stream fish, but they are caught in little riffles or broad Canadian rivers and sometimes come up from great depths to leap clear of the water as they take a floating fly. Although it frequently leaps when hooked, the grayling lacks the fighting power of most trouts.

Although grayling are caught on all sorts of flies, both imitations of natural insects and gaudy imitations of nothing, they feed largely on other water life, mainly shrimp-like creatures in waters of low fertility by most standards. In large lakes, shoals

134

*Fish census (below) is taken by team
of biologists using electrical shocking gear in
western trout stream. Boat camp
for fishermen on western lake. Irrigation
is hazard of trout streams where
water is diverted from main rivers and taken
through ditches to valley crops.
Bulldozers build temporary dams and canals
to draw off flow in dry season.*

of grayling are sometimes sighted along the shorelines, often appearing to be inactive and resting.

Not only is the grayling sensitive to many of the things that even a trout would ignore, but growth is slow and the individual fish does not spawn every year. So a planted population is an uncertain thing and the outcome may remain in doubt for several years.

It is in the propagation and distribution of salmons that fisheries biologists have their greatest success today and a chance to recoup some of man's clumsy losses. Salmon introductions have no record of harmful results. And in the Great Lakes, man has achieved a triumph that followed one of the worst debacles in fish management.

Some of the problem began with construction of the Welland Canal, which passed water life from Lake Ontario into the other lakes. Until then, Niagara Falls had been an effective barrier. But now the parasitic sea lamprey came through the canal and into the upper Great Lakes. It spread slowly. It was years before it began to take its heavy toll of lake trout, herring, turbot, and whitefish. With the lamprey came the alewife, a fish resembling a small shad, which also prospered in enormous numbers. White perch came as well, not a welcome addition to a confused situation, but less harmful than the other immigrants.

The lampreys attached themselves to lake trout and by the middle nineteen-fifties sport and commercial fishing were at a low ebb. Ninety percent of the Great Lakes' fish population was made up of the ubiquitous alewives.

The lake trout is a particularly vulnerable species because of its slow growth and thin distribution. The deep, cold waters it chooses do not support large numbers of fish, and once it was assailed by the lamprey it had no protection. The lamprey had left its natural predators behind and its long life cycle (the young may spend ten years as mud-dwelling creatures) made the problem more complex. Finally, a selective poison was developed to kill the juveniles in spawning streams. Then fish managers looked about for a game fish to harvest the hordes of alewives. Pacific salmon proved to be the answer.

The coho or silver salmon is a different fish to different fishermen. In the Pacific it cruises in schools, sometimes at great depth, sometimes on the surface, especially in estuaries. In offshore waters it may be caught by deep trolling. Then, as it gathers about river mouths to begin its upstream journey, it is often vulnerable to lures cast with light tackle and to shallow trolling.

A few miles from the ocean a fisherman works a little creek the way he would fish for trout, using a light spinning rod and small lures, and when the silver salmon strikes the battle seems inappropriate to so small a waterway. In some such streams fly tackle can be used, and many steelhead anglers catch silvers together with big rainbow trout. The silver changes, however, even in its first few miles of upstream travel. The fins are marked in yellow tints, an early sign of spawning and of death. Only one who has known the fish well will notice, but already the flesh is a bit softer and the fish's power is waning.

The coho or silver does not undertake the long river migrations of the chinook, and because it usually spawns no great distance inland from the coast, it suffers less from upstream damming. It does not wander great distances at sea, but lives in the general area of its home river.

*Coho or silver salmon have brought
revolutionary fishing to much of America as
propagation became successful
in Great Lakes area. Coho were originally found
only on America's West Coast, where
they provided much of the commercial fishery.
Available to light-tackle anglers
in streams (opposite), the coho spawns only once
and thorough harvest is encouraged.*

Michigan received the first coho eggs in 1965, and the smolts weighed an ounce when they were stocked in the spring of 1966. No natural reproduction was expected, but the smolts were planted in rivers from which they could reach open water. By 1967 the fish, fattened on alewives, were being caught in great numbers, averaging nearly fifteen pounds.

There were human complications as new anglers found themselves confronted by an abundance of large fish, not too hard to catch, and they went offshore in all kinds of boats, many unsuited to rough water. Storms took a heavy toll before the boat sizes and designs were upgraded to meet Lake Michigan's seas. Most Great Lakes coho are caught by trolling and the depth is critical, for the fish tend to stratify at suitable temperatures. Electronic equipment was used to find the schools of fish and "breakaway" trolling gear enabled fishermen to get their lures to the proper depth and then to play a catch on a free line after the heavy weight needed to reach the proper depth was uncoupled with the strike. Other states bordering the Great Lakes began coho programs of their own. Introductions also worked with other Pacific salmons, as well as with steelhead and brown trout.

There were problems of coho management, even after success was achieved. Sport fishermen with light tackle promptly learned that some of the migrating fish could be caught in the rivers they migrated through, especially near the river mouths. But others felt snagging the fish was just as much pleasure and certainly more productive. Snagging and light-tackle casting are hardly compatible in close quarters and under most conditions the snagging would have been restrained, but in the case of the salmon there was little valid argument against harvesting all of the fish possible. They would die and be wasted if allowed to continue up the rivers, and they would not spawn successfully. The supply is maintained artifically.

Fishermen meet the sea by casting
from high bridges where pilings form shade and
sanctuary for a variety of salt-water
species. Bridge anglers can be highly skilled in
learning locations of feeding fish
as tide and light change. Surf fishermen push to
farthest points of wave-battered rocks
to cast to bluefish, which swing near shore on
swift feeding forays in broken water.

Now the Great Lakes are seen in all of their environmental complexity, the necessity for an alleviation of pollution is plain, and the final outcome of current management projects depends on variables not fully understood. Management has never before been directed at such immense bodies of water.

THE CLOUD TROUT

Fishermen are adventurers and travelers, and the reasons for their journeys are not necessarily more fish, or even bigger fish, but often a desire for a unique setting or an unmarred wilderness. The high-mountain angler leaves the valleys for the labors of the trail, the frugal camp, and jeweled snow lakes with their bright residents and wild neighbors.

The horses are mounted near a broad river in fertile farmland, a river of slow and glassy pools where the trout rises appear as placid circles in evening, and of choppy rapids where a quick, small fish's rush at an insect is hardly noticed. In midsummer the river is low and a Canada goose with her obedient procession of goslings moves slowly along the borders of marshy backwaters. Whitetail deer walk there in late evening, moving out from the brush that has hidden them through the warm day.

There are large trout in the big river and as the little packtrain forms and begins to move uncertainly, creaking and thumping in the early morning, the travelers see an occasional splash of moving fish. Sunlight comes late because of snow-blotched peaks in the east, but it erases the morning chill in minutes once it reaches the valley floor. The fishermen turn their backs on the river and begin a gradual ascent.

The trail narrows beside a swift tributary that batters its way between and over giant boulders, slowing only in short, foamy pools where the fishermen have caught plump trout on other days, but the horses continue upward with occasional grunts at the logs they must cross, logs that have come down the canyon in early spring floods. The trail then goes above the noisy water, probing through heavy pine forest and across grassy parks brilliant with new flowers. But the sound of the plunging creek is heard for most of the morning. At a rest stop the fishermen hear the snap of a twig somewhere above them, but the animal that breaks it is unseen and unidentified. In a muddy spot on the trail are tracks of mule deer and of a single elk. Canada jays observe the laboring procession with curiosity, and tiny pine squirrels chirk in complaint and scuttle about on low branches.

By noon there are rotting snow patches on the north side of boulders, and when the horses drink in a high meadow brook the riders see darting shadows of alarmed trout that quickly disappear, each fish finding a favorite hiding place it probably has used many times before. The trail crosses boggy areas that once were beaver ponds and now show signs of Shiras moose, and more recent constructions hold wide pools dimpled by small fish.

It is midafternoon when the timber becomes skimpier and some trees are wind-twisted and dwarfed. By then the air is thin and the rest stops are frequent. The grass has given way to subalpine growth, almost tundra, and when the little lake is reached it appears suddenly, a pocket fed by trickling snow water from cliffs higher up. It is almost at a mountaintop, hardly a hundred yards across, and its center is dark blue. Its borders are a lighter shade because of the shelving bottom. It tapers at the upper end where there is a miniature marsh, and a small overflow at the

140

other end is the beginning of a tiny creek that will be joined by other brooks to form the roaring stream followed early in the day.

The boulders about the little lake's edge are sharp-edged instead of rounded like those of the valley river, and some of them are submerged. As the age of stones is measured these are new boulders. The camp is a simple one. Its little tents are erected quickly from long practice and the evening meal is assembled over a miniature fire that sends its bluish smoke straight up toward a bright sky. The lake is already in shadow when the fishermen extract their gear from the panniers and string the light rods, sectioned for packing convenience.

One of the fishermen stands beside a boulder, so that for a trout his outline will be broken, and he studies the gradual bottom slope formed by centuries of slow erosion from the lake's bank. A short cast away the bottom becomes vague and fades into the blue of deeper water. The light is failing and it is hard to make out details, but the fisherman believes he sees movement there and he carefully strips line from his reel and takes a last look behind him to be sure there is room for his backcast. But before he begins it he sees a fish in plain sight only a few feet away on the light bottom, and he wonders how it could have gotten there without attracting his attention. The fish is no more than ten inches long, but it is so near that its bright color is plain, even in the dull light. He does not cast but waits for it to move farther away so he will not startle it. It turns toward the deep water and glides off, becoming fainter as it goes until it disappears entirely.

The angler straightens his line smoothly and casts toward the drop-off, his small, dark fly striking like a raindrop and sinking quickly out of sight on its eight feet of slender leader. When he has waited a few seconds he twitches his fly line gently with his fingers and begins to retrieve it slowly while watching where the leader enters the water. He senses suddenly that the fly has stopped and he lifts the fragile rod tip almost involuntarily with his wrist to feel the fish's tug. He draws it toward him, seeing the fish darting in short runs over the light bottom.

His catch has required no great skill and it is not a large brook trout, but it has the bright colors and hard body of high-country fish and he grins happily at his prize. He is no novice angler and there are much larger fish he can take in the broad valley river. There are other fish he can catch in the roaring tributary of the canyon only a short walk up the trail, but he has come a long, hard way for this one. He does not know who put the brook trout there or when it was done. He knows that there is a sheer falls not far below the little lake, and that if someone had not carried its ancestors there he would have no fish to catch. But in this, the most remote fishing place he knows of, the brook trout has been in residence for a long while, brought by someone of another year or another decade. He holds the icy trout in his hand, loosens the fly gently and wonders if there is another lake in the notch a little above him. If there is, he thinks, he might be able to take a few fish there in a canvas bucket. Or had someone already done that?

BALCONY AT SEA

They received less attention than those who went farther out, but coastal fishermen began to find new places for their feet and bait buckets as new highway bridges, spurred on by noisy automobiles in the new century, began to cross coastal rivers. And there appeared a structure for the fisherman himself, the fishing pier, a balcony that went to sea and took the boatless angler farther than any surfman could cast. It was an imposing structure compared to the narrow stands used by the tycoons who had pursued striped bass in an earlier day, and although it was easily manned by novices the fishing pier fostered its own expert fishermen.

The piers grew, often as civic enterprises, from resort cities and sometimes from bathing beaches, and they intercepted the marauding droves of bluefish, the sweeping tours of mackerel, and the schools of red drum that sometimes turned the swells golden. Almost any inshore fish could be caught from a pier, from Pacific yellowtail to moody cobia that made spring migrations along the shores of the Gulf of Mexico and the eastern coast. The pier is an outpost of information and news of a run moves along the grapevine and can bring a crowd. When the fish are in, the rails will be crowded, and sometimes remarkably silent, as anglers concentrate upon their baits and the lines of their neighbors. There are special techniques for an angler high above water, and there are lures specially made to keep their level attitude while being retrieved from above.

And the pier attracts its own resident population, generally lesser fishes, for its aging pilings collect barnacles and give hiding to bait-fish that feed on smaller things about the structure. There is shade in sunny weather and when the storms come the pier demolishes some of the waves and creates its own pattern of current and runouts. The flounder fisherman bends with the rail pressing his waistline, and where the sheepshead is present there are fishing specialists who concentrate on infinitesimal twitches of their lines.

Not all of the resident fish are small. There may be sharks beneath the pier or near it, and barracuda have lived for years at some piers, evidently replacing their hooked predecessors automatically. Florida piers often have their destructive snook that cut lines on piling barnacles, and weakfish stay for considerable periods around some piers before moving on. So the pier is a fishing community with visiting fish and fishermen, but a residential quota of both.

Harbor and inlet improvements brought the jetty, a wave-pounded vantage point for anglers who defy occasional breakers and are often bruised on rocks and cut by barnacles. Some of them wear cleated boots for their task and have specially built tackle for their precarious perches. The inlets are patterns of strong currents, tidal rips, depths and shallows, feeding their brackish waters into the saltier depths, carrying a multitude of water life with their discharge. The jetty jockey, like most other anglers, is likely to be a specialist with mental tidal charts and secret knowledge of shoals and eddies. The expert stands beside fishless novices and fills his burlap bag with weakfish or pompano.

Coastal fishes were observed more closely as the twentieth century wore on and their patterns began to appear in scholarly works. For hundreds of years anglers had employed crude methods of tagging their catches, but the process began to take organized form with the cooperation of both sport and commercial fishermen.

Deep-sea sports angling came with the end of the nineteenth century and its very nature attracted wealthy and prominent men willing to probe a new subject. It gradually became evident that fish management could some day be extended to the sea itself.

7. New Quarry.

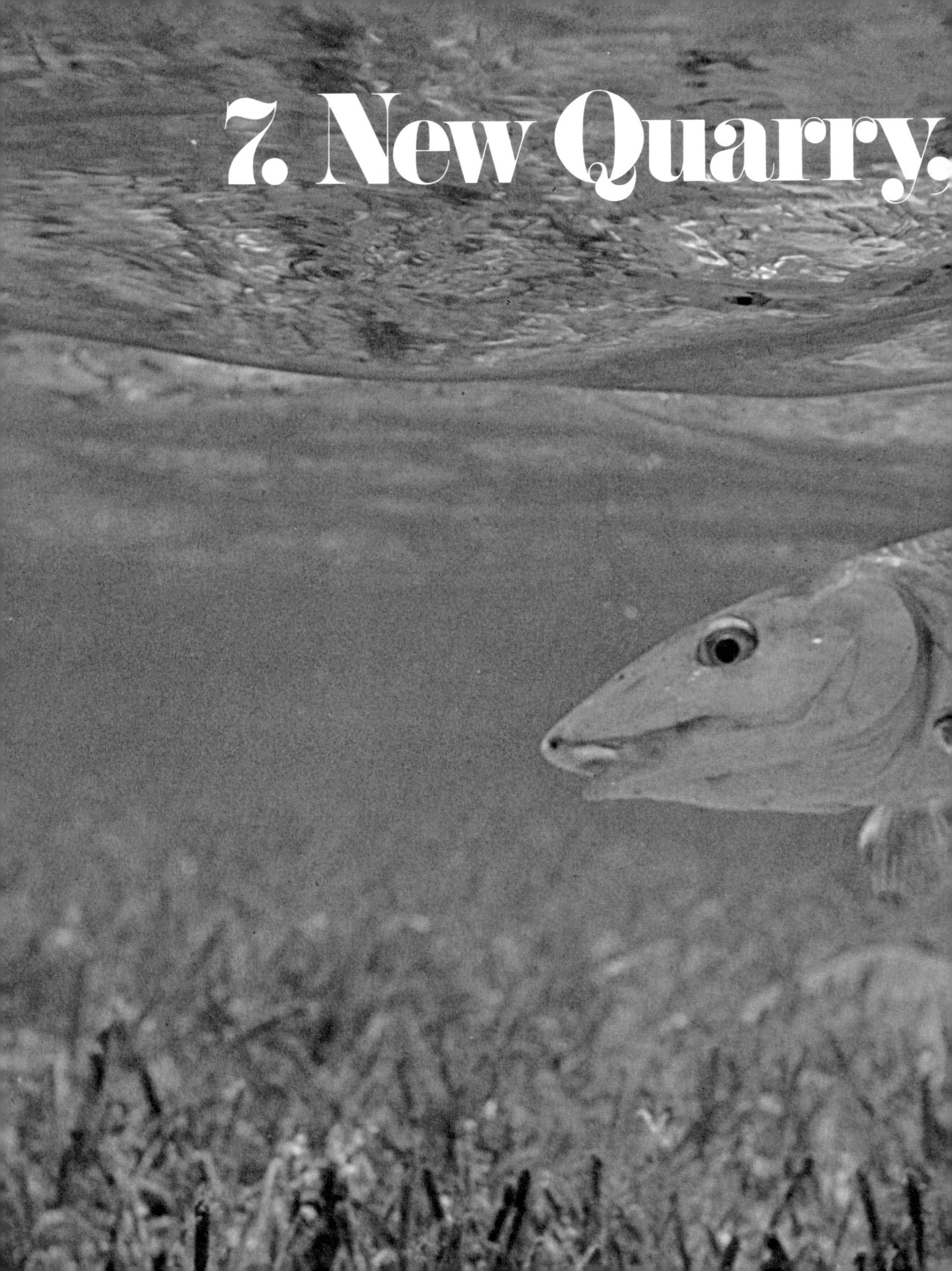

New Anglers

Charles Frederick Holder of Pasadena caught a 183-pound bluefin tuna on rod and reel off Catalina Island on June 1, 1898. San Juan Hill was taken by American forces in Cuba a month later and American salt-water anglers seemed to attach equal importance to the events.

Holder's fishing triumph was the beginning of an era, for it proved that true deep-water fish could be handled on sporting tackle and it opened the seven seas to those who could afford the new game. The fact that others had caught tuna on rod and reel before Holder did not detract from the fish's importance, for it was Holder's catch that received the publicity. It is likely that his was the largest fish caught to that date. It was the beginning of the Catalina Tuna Club and of deep-sea angling.

W. E. Wood's tarpon, and others that came after it, had proved the tackle would handle large fish, but the tarpon is a leaper and lives in shallow water where he cannot sound in the final test of tackle and fisherman. The tuna makes long runs, swims at high speed, has great power, and will go deep.

The tackle used for tuna, as described by Holder, included a reel with a drag that prevented overrunning, but the heavy braking was provided by a leather thumb device. Such reels held about two hundred feet of 21-thread linen line and were used with rods of around seven feet with agate guides and a long butt.

Holder was the son of Dr. J. B. Holder, who was prominent in eastern scholarly circles and a founder of the American Museum of Natural History in New York. Young Holder had come to California at the age of thirty-four, after considerable fishing experience which included several years of residence in the Florida Keys. In California he served as editor of the Los Angeles *Tribune*, founded and edited a magazine, *California Illustrated*, and wrote a book on zoology. His fight with the big tuna took three hours and forty-five minutes, and at one time the boat capsized, but Holder and his guide, Jim Gardner, managed to board it again and continue the fray.

The Catalina Tuna Club was established for fishermen who had caught California tuna weighing at least a hundred pounds with rod and reel and using line no stronger than 24-thread (72-pound test). Club membership grew rapidly, and all catches were so well publicized that deep-sea fishing attracted wealthy men all over the world. The buttons worn by members to indicate their catches could have been the beginning of formal competitive angling at sea, and an authoritative British angling writer, Frederick G. Aflalo, said after visiting the club that "the inordinate thirst for buttons does much to spoil the true spirit of sport." But deep-sea accomplishments continued to be measured and weighed, and the catcher of large fish remains a competitor.

In the beginning of deep-sea sport fishing there were no rows of manned cruisers to be chartered by the day. The pioneers of the sport were men able to outfit their own boats or maintain their own exclusive clubs. As such they were colorful; they had chosen a new sport and accepted the hardship and frustration that came with it. The Catalina Tuna Club was joined by a good share of the first deepwater anglers, the best-known of whom was Zane Grey, the successful author of western novels that made him rich and famous. They continue to sell; other writers' themes may be more sophisticated, but cannot capture the timeless appeal of *Riders of the Purple Sage* or *The*

Opening pages: Bonefish, prize of the salt flats, is tenderly released by one of its admirers. Light tackle made it a challenge to expert anglers. Bonefish did not become popular until fly and spinning tackle had been adapted to shallow salt water. Zane Grey (below) was pioneer of deep-sea angling and scorned some of early club regulations.

146

*Tired bonefish is brought to hand
by fly-fisherman wading on shallow flat. After
anglers learned to play the gray
ghost on a light drag they found its runs were not
endless after all. Bonefishing
is a form of hunting with fishing tackle, the fish
usually being sighted before the
cast is made. Knowledge of routes and tidal
movements are guide's stock in trade.*

Light of Western Stars. Zane Grey wrote of a brief span of western history that was already gone, but his romantic view of it and his sense of the dramatic were qualities that also sent him in pursuit of giant fish. His melodramatic accounts of adventures with great fish made enemies among contemporary anglers who felt he was overstating his case, but those colorful tales caused some later fishermen to insist his relatively unknown "fish stories" were much better than his western sagas.

He was born in Zanesville, Ohio, as Pearl Gray, a name which inevitably involved him in youthful combat with tormentors until he changed to Zane, after some illustrious ancestors on his mother's side. He was an ardent angler from childhood on and attended the University of Pennsylvania on a baseball scholarship. He began a dental career in New York, but abruptly ended it to become a writer of outdoor stories. When his success as an author of westerns was assured, Grey (he changed the spelling, too) began searching the world for big fish. For some time, beginning in 1914, he made his summer headquarters at Catalina and he became a competitive member of the Tuna Club. His disagreements with other fishermen and his lurid accounts of his own achievements caused him to be derided by some angling writers, but he contributed greatly to the sport, especially through his long expeditions to foreign waters.

Some of the friction between Grey and other anglers was owing to his strong feelings about tackle. For one thing, he continually preached suiting the tackle to the fish and did not believe in what might be known as "stunt" fishing in a later day. He was also contemptuous of some of the rules followed by the Tuna Club, many of which were found necessary long afterward in establishing records.

Grey was a conservationist and preached the use of sporting gear. He endeavored to get anglers away from the hand line and his obsession with billfish did much to open that branch of the sport. The broadbill swordfish became his favorite quarry and he established effective methods for it. W. C. Boschen, another member of the club, joined him in his broadbill interests. Boschen, an older and more experienced fisherman, caught a world-record broadbill of 463 pounds in 1917, but Grey belittled the catch because the fish had been hooked in the heart and his friendship with Boschen was strained. Grey hoped to turn the major interests of the club from tuna to broadbill. When he caught a 418-pound broadbill in 1920, his stirring accounts of the battle cost him friends at the club but it was a woman member's catch which finally separated him from the organization. The woman, slightly-built Mrs. Keith Spalding, landed a 426-pound broadbill in 1921, and when other members teased Grey on the subject he said she could not have landed the fish without help. That led to an open break with the Catalina group and Grey's resignation.

Grey took his big-fish angling very seriously, exercised to keep in shape for the battles, and toughened his hands for the work, but he was not impressed by rules against broken lines, broken rods, and assistance on the rod. His purpose was to land the fish and if it were a combined effort he told it that way. It was true that patching a broken rod or splicing a bad line during a fight might be more difficult than landing a fish with whole equipment, but there must be restrictions to give meaning to records. In Grey's day those were not well established.

Grey caught a world-record blue-

fin tuna off Nova Scotia and initiated broadbill sword-fishing in New Zealand waters. He caught an enormous record-breaking blue marlin off Tahiti, landed giant sharks off Australia, and was still planning long expeditions at his death in 1939. His younger brother, R. C., accompanied him on many of his trips, landed his share of the catches, and was persuaded by Zane to write a book about his own experiences.

Some of the big-game fishing of Grey's day was truly dangerous, since the boats were often in strange waters and methods of handling giant swordfish and marlin were in their infancy. Even so, the agonies of effort described in his colorful prose seemed somewhat exaggerated to a fishing public used to news accounts of World War I. In *Tales of Fishes*, 1919, he tells of two fights with swordfish, beginning with a fish hooked at Avalon in 1916. In accepted form, the boat's captain had circled a surfaced swordfish that displayed a "huge, brown leathery tail and dorsal fin," and had drawn the flying-fish bait into position for the strike.

After holding the fish for four hours, the angler found his reel was freezing "just as my other one had frozen on my first swordfish," and he suggested to the captain that they run slack into the line, cut it and attach it to another reel. The captain stated that would disqualify the fish for the Tuna Club records.

Grey quotes himself with the response, "I am using regulation tackle and to my mind the more tackle we use, provided we land the fish, the more credit is due us. It is not an easy matter to change reels or lines or rods with a big fish working all the time."

He then states for his readers:

"Captain Dan [Danielson], like all the boatmen at Avalon, has fixed ideas about the Tuna Club and its records and requirements. It is all right, I suppose, for a club to have rules, and not count or credit an angler who breaks a rod or is driven to the expedient I had proposed. But I do not fish for clubs or records. I fish for the fun, the excitement, the thrill of the game, and I would rather let my fish go than not."

At any rate the line was cut and spliced to another reel that day, and when Grey pulled "until I saw stars and my bones cracked" the rod broke at the reel and bent the reel seat. The reel was hammered off and placed in another butt.

Grey describes his condition: "I was burning all over; wet and slippery, and aching in every muscle. These next few minutes seemed longer than all the hours. I found to put the old strain on the rod made me blind with pain.... Here I was in agony, absolutely useless. Why did I keep it up? I could not give up and I concluded I was crazy....I sweat, I panted, I whistled, I bled—and my arms were dead, and my hands raw and my heart seemed about to burst."

The hook pulled out of that swordfish. A few days later, the blisters on his hands not completely healed, Grey was hooked to another broadbill and this time he used a fighting harness. He found he could lift the fish much better, but cracked his big Conroy rod. They splinted the rod and the splints broke. Grey gave up and allowed the boat captain to play the fish, although when it was alongside the double line snapped.

It was such accounts that drew sarcastic comments from other big-game fishermen of his time, but a later generation of anglers, realizing the exaggeration but appreciative of the difficulties en-

*Striped marlin leaps wildly
near fishing cruiser in Sea of Cortez, Mexico.
Modern anglers cover the world and find
suitable equipment almost everywhere game fish are
located. Sailfish is brought aboard
modern sportfisherman with high vantage points
for crew's lookout activities. Big
dolphin fights to the last against ceaseless
pressure of angler's line.*

Toothy barracuda is landed by caster in shallow water. Large specimens are found at edge of shallow flats in warm-water seas. Speed of retrieve is factor in barracuda fishing and rapid trolling may be most effective method. Careful handling is essential with barracuda; teeth are dangerous. The fish sometimes destroys hooked catches of other game species.

countered with tackle which must be considered experimental for such tasks, read Grey's "fish stories" with relish.

The Danielson boat from which Grey fished on those days was a thirty-eight-footer, equipped with both sail and engine. Some of the boats which he himself owned were more pretentious. The Depression of the thirties found him with a sail and motor yacht manufactured for Kaiser Wilhelm II. It proved to be too expensive, however, even for Grey.

The baiting of swordfish was a new skill at the time and their habit of lying or "finning" on the surface made a high vantage point helpful. Grey used a crow's-nest rigged on a mast high above the water. Although he hooked fish from there he would then take the rod to a fighting chair in the cockpit.

Kite fishing, an ancient art of primitive land-based fishermen, was revived at the Catalina Tuna Club through the ingenuity of Captain George Farnesworth. Tuna of the area had demonstrated they were boat-shy, and by use of a kite Farnesworth was able to present his flying-fish bait far from the cockpit. The bait was suspended between the soaring kite and the boat and it could be jumped and dipped at the surface through rod manipulation. The Catalina tuna, which later faded from the angling scene, were leaping fish when chasing bait on the surface, and their boat shyness was contrary to the behavior of many other tuna, some of which are attracted by a sport-fisherman's wake.

The rods were likely to break and the reels, although they had star-drags early in the twentieth century, were still likely to give trouble on long runs with heavy braking. The teaser was finding favor as a means of attracting fish to hooked bait.

The waters about Catalina changed rapidly and became crowded with commercial fishing boats even when Grey fished there. In 1917 he reported one hundred and thirty-two Japanese boats at one time. Using anchovy baits the Japanese chummed schools of albacore that were sighted on the surface, drew them to the boat's stern, and hooked them on baited barbless hooks. Although at that time the Japanese had not learned to catch tuna, Grey prophesied they would soon do so. The Japanese commercial operators drove the tuna schools down out of reach of the sporting anglers and broadbill swordfish were skillfully harpooned by the Japanese.

Grey was especially bitter about the round-haul nets used by commercial fishermen, nets that worked two hundred feet deep and "must be a mile long." The albacore supply dwindled and in 1918 the market fishermen found a way to net large tuna with longer and deeper nets. The broadbills apparently left with the albacore. The Pacific was changing, even as the Atlantic and the inland waters were, and it was the blue-water anglers who lamented it first.

The men who began deep-sea angling were unusual in their wealth, their desire to go farther for bigger fish, and their competition with the sea, the fish and with each other.

THE SHALLOW FLATS

Discovery of the bonefish took many years, or perhaps it was an unending series of discoveries by different anglers, each of whom told his personal story as a revelation to the world, often ignoring the experiences of earlier "discoverers."

No game fish had been sur-

rounded by so much confusion as to identification and characteristics. There were excellent illustrations of the bonefish and the ladyfish or ten-pounder, but the names were hopelessly confused and both were described as great leapers, even by the usually reliable Dr. Henshall. The ladyfish jumps and the bonefish does not. Early accounts of jumping went with illustrations depicting the bonefish, regardless of the name it went by, and the errors have never been explained. By 1896 there were accurate descriptions of the bonefish's runs on the Florida flats, even though some anglers still considered it a mystery fish.

Bonefish are the leading representatives of a special kind of fishing, that of shallow water in which the fish is seen before a cast is made,

and it is one of the most recent techniques. Its stronghold in America is the Florida Keys and sport anglers had worked its area for a hundred years before they developed methods that realized its potential.

Fumbling efforts by beginning bonefishermen with inappropriate tackle are exemplified by those of Zane Grey and his brother, R. C., in 1919. Like a great many other expert anglers, they had tried to defeat the Ghost of the Flats with little help from more experienced fishermen. Grey's report is not one of method development but of hyperbole and frustration. Believing a fish that averaged no more than four pounds should be worked with light tackle, they used black-bass equipment and eighteen-pound test line with crabmeat for bait, and approached the game with what

*Master angler Stu Apte brings
100-pound tarpon to boat with fly rod. Fish will be
lip-gaffed and released. Fly-fishing
for giant salt-water fish has been perfected in
recent years. Early tarpon anglers
thought no rod and reel could land the silver
king. Inshore barracuda is gaffed
in photo at right. Oil rigs in Gulf of Mexico
provide shelter for variety of fish.*

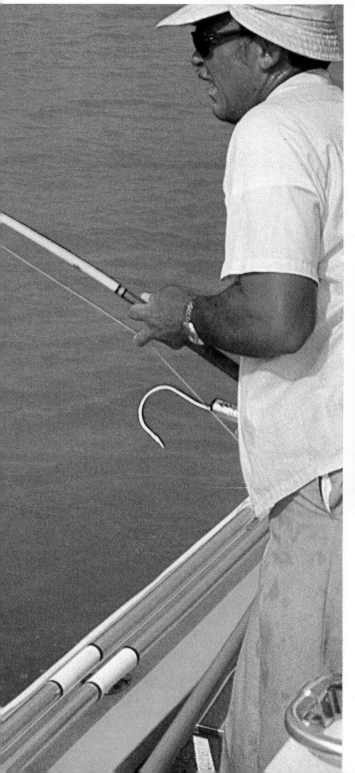

*Ocean perch is taken by spinning
gear on Washington coast. Surf-fishermen of
Gulf of California use hand-crafted
beach buggy to cover coastline.
Big yellowtail, swift favorite of West
Coast anglers, is gaffed off Baja. Giant black
sea bass (lower right) requires
two gaff hooks. Two-hundred-pounder is a prize
for deep-water bottom-fishing.*

Surf-caster with giant spinning rod
probes breakers near old pilings. Surfman
is a hardy member of the angling
fraternity, practicing his sport day and night
and competing with harsh weather
and smashing surf, as well as with the fish.
Surf-fishing as it is known today
was developed following World War II and is
now hampered by beach development.

Grey called "the innocence of our hearts and assurance of our vanity." When they lost innumerable hooked fish in months of effort, Grey concluded that the bonefish was the "wisest, shyest, wariest and strangest" fish he had ever encountered. Much of their effort was still-fishing and they were unable to cast without heavy sinkers. Delicacy of presentation was impossible and they did not mention fly rods.

In deep water, where it is occasionally caught, the bonefish is a strong yet not unusual performer, but on the thin water of shining flats its speed is magnified. It does not go as fast as Zane Grey, or many that came after him, believed, but its smoking trail of stirred marl has made fishermen guess seventy miles an hour. The hooking of a bonefish is a process of building tension, beginning when the fish is but a questionable shadow in the distance. The quarry may be recognized while still out of casting range, and then the angler tries to plan his cast and guess the fish's speed. It is hunting over water, and some anglers favor it above all other sport.

The first bonefish were caught on bait, with heavy tackle, and they broke surprisingly strong gear. But the first bonefishermen had not learned that the fish can be handled on a light drag if it is allowed to run. In fact, they lacked the right equipment; proper bonefishing waited for smooth drags on fly, spinning, or plugging reels, and for rods that would throw very light things for seventy-five feet or more and drop them gently ahead of a cautious fish.

Bonefish are caught by casting into the clouds of mud they have stirred in their bottom feeding. They can be hooked when lured near a boat by judiciously drifted ground chum, and they can be stalked when their tails and fins glint above water that cannot cover them. Others are cast to as they move slowly across flats singly or in schools, or "pods," an action demanding accurate casting and careful judgment of speed and behavior.

The fly-fisherman for bonefish stands high on his skiff while a poler slides the boat along with a building tide, placing his pole as silently as possible. Where the water is very shallow the keel rubs lightly on turtle grass. The flat that was almost dry an hour before sparkles with a foot of water in its deeper places and partly submerges the shoreline mangrove roots bared at low tide.

The angler sees his fish as a slow movement over the blotchy bottom some distance away and identifies it instantly although he has also seen bonnet sharks, barracuda, and small rays. He holds his cast until the proper moment and makes it with an economy of motion, the line roping out to drop the fly in the fish's path, only a few feet ahead of it, and when the fish has reached the proper point he lifts his rod tip slightly and lowers it again, so that his fly will hop a little, like a tiny, frightened crab.

The fish is close enough that the angler can see it plainly. He notes the quickened motion of its tail as it sights the fly, glides toward it, and tips down to find the fly on the bottom. Half of its tail and a tall fin show above the water as it takes the thing into its small mouth. As it turns slightly there is a delicate tightening of the line. The fisherman sets his small, sharp hook briskly. For an instant the fish pauses, puzzled. Then it streaks across the flat toward deep water, leaving a boil of gray mud behind it. The extra line hisses through the guides briefly before the fish is "on the reel" and the angler lifts his tip to clear as much water as possible. The reel runs smoothly with a

*King, or chinook, salmon (above)
is top catch for both commercial and sports
anglers of West Coast. Deep trolling
is favorite sport method when fish are offshore.
Migration of salmon brings migration
of fishermen to mouth of Oregon's Klamath River.
When fish are making upstream run
small boats guard their route and shore anglers
can cast to path of moving fish.*

Acrobatic steelhead has become the
glamour fish of the West. It is a rainbow trout
that goes to sea, returning as
a silvery fighter to be caught in rocky rivers and
in placid creeks. It has prompted
special tackle and skills. Methods adapted
to steelhead that run deep in muddy
winter flows are widely different from tactics
used when waters are clear and low.

light drag; the procedure is almost routine, but it is a studied series of moves the first bonefishermen took a long time to perfect.

Although line melts swiftly from the spool, the fisherman lets it go. The fish runs in a series of bursts that carries it more than a hundred yards and to the edge of deeper water. There it pauses, and short tugs on the line tell that it is trying to root out the fly on the bottom. It then goes in a wide circle and the rod is pushed up at arm's length so the line and backing will clear abrasive sea fans and coral. Several shorter runs follow, but when the fisherman reaches down to release the fish it is paddling weakly on its side. To be certain it will recover, he moves it a few times with his hand on the wrist of its tail.

Altogether it is a simple process, but hard-learned and precise. It was not until after World War II that bonefishing really boomed and attracted sportsmen from all over the world. The shallows of the Florida Keys and the Caribbean became some of the most prized fishing waters of the world and boats and tackle were fitted to them.

There are many other fish on the flats, and most of them perform very differently from the way they do in the comparative safety of deeper water. Even the red drum or channel bass, generally a deep tugger, runs swiftly when the water is shallow. The permit, hardly known before it was found in clear shallows, is a broad-sided speedster, seldom caught there with artificial lures, but occasionally prey to small jigs or streamers. The barracuda, often in heroic sizes, plies the edges of deep water, and on the flats the tarpon finally became a light-tackle target, although first it was caught in deeper channels on heavier gear. The flats are for daintier presentations.

NEW THINGS IN DEEP WATER

Deep-sea fishing began as a means of hooking giants, but its techniques produced other kinds of fishing, incidental at first, but eventually as popular as the main objective. Fish such as the dolphin, several kinds of jacks, and the lesser tunas became prized game for lighter tackle. They were fished generally as a sideline, but often as the main objective on offshore trips.

Dolphin fishing with light tackle is a good example, the dolphin moving over the blue waters far from shore. Although some dolphin of more than eighty pounds have been caught, most of them are much smaller, and the "chicken" dolphin has provided sport for anglers using equipment suited to pike or black bass.

In or near the Gulf Stream, the Atlantic sportfisherman trolls briskly, his rigged baits skipping on the waves near a floating weed line and causing white streaks of bubbles when they are drawn under. Such baits may attract a wide variety of fish, but the dolphin caster uses them primarily to bring his quarry close enough to be reached with other tackle. The small "school dolphin" flash and leap about the large baits, and when one is hooked the engines are stopped and the boat lies dead in the water while a fisherman throws to the crowded survivors with the first catch left in the water.

A mate scatters chum from the transom and the angler catches fish with gear appropriate for the occasion. The dolphin may be less than five pounds, but they demonstrate the same leaps and runs of their larger brethren and are willing game.

Small tunas, it was found, could be attracted to offshore fishing boats by chumming, and almost anything might appear in the sparkling path of

*Steelhead weather (below) is likely
to be cold and wet. This fish came from Green
River in Washington. Of all sea-run
trouts, steelhead is believed to make longest sea
journeys. Instinct for the sea is
bred into steelhead, but their appearance in youth
is same as that of other rainbows.
Spinfisherman (opposite) fights leaping steelie
near treacherous river snag.*

chum streamed back from an anchored or drifting boat. Amberjack and some of their close relatives were brought up from wrecks and bottom boulders, the feeding stripes bright on their heads, evidently ready to attack almost anything offered. Thus the light-tackle enthusiast benefited from the learning of those who sought swordfish and giant bluefin tuna.

The flying bridge developed as a lookout post for the captain of an offshore craft, a second set of controls mounted high above the cockpit, and from it he could look for surfacing fish, watch the behavior of his trolled baits, and learn the actions of hooked fish even before the angler knew of them. By the thirties it was an accepted feature of sport-fishing cruisers. Then came the tuna tower—popular by the nineteen-fifties—a crow's-nest far above even the flying bridge. At first it was no more than a lookout station, but controls were eventually installed, making three levels from which the boat could be maneuvered.

Harlan Major (1889-1968), a tackle dealer in southern California and later a fishing writer and a successful promotor of fishing from Long Island to Chile, was a developer of the modern fishing chair. Major did not claim to have invented it, but he recognized that the punishment absorbed in fighting large fish was due largely to improper bracing and improper distribution of strain against the rod. Early catches of giant fish often resulted in physical injury to the fishermen, and the first harnesses worn by rod men actually were considered dangerous. With the modern adjustable chair, which swings easily to face the hooked fish, and a well-fitted harness, some of the pain has gone out of the sport. Major said many of the early chairs were so poorly designed that the fishermen "skidded around the seat like butter on a hot plate."

The first seats were simply ordinary office models fastened down, but Major and others with mechanical know-how changed that in the thirties.

Outriggers put the trolled bait well to the side of the boat's course, enabled more lines to be used, and handled heavy baits that would have exerted excessive pull on the fisherman's rod. It was a long way from the cedar poles and hand lines for pickerel trolling to the outriggers that attracted billfish in the Gulf Stream, but the principle was the same. To get the baits clear of boat's wake, bamboo poles were extensively used at first. Tommy Gifford, a legendary offshore captain who began his career just after World War I, came forth in 1934 with metal outriggers that were nearly forty-five feet long.

In a restless career Gifford spanned the Atlantic Coast, the Caribbean, and some of the Pacific, and his insight as a charterman put him in the employ of many of the leading anglers of his time—some of whom became fast friends and some of whom he referred to with acid resentment. Gifford was headstrong and violent in his likes and dislikes, but before his death in 1970 no one ever doubted that he was one of the great offshore fishermen who ever lived. His clients—among them Michael Lerner, Kip Farrington, Harlan Major, Ernest Hemingway, and Van Campen Heilner—continually set records. He found fault with the big-game reels of his day and his ideas were later incorporated in modern ones, although the designs involved so many fishermen that their development cannot be credited to anyone.

Shortly after World War II a completely new kind of salt-water sport fishing evolved as a side effect of an activity conservationists viewed with apprehension. This was oil-rig fishing. Offshore

*Bait-casting tackle is used to land
fresh-run king salmon. Angler Erwin Bauer uses
chest waders. Chinook salmon
deteriorates rapidly as it proceeds upstream to
spawning areas and silver sheen
is lost as death approaches. Sporting tackle is at
its best near river mouths, where fish
have vigor of the sea but are forced into shallow
water and established routes.*

oil wells and their attendant structures provided enormous artificial reefs in the Gulf of Mexico, often a long way from shore. When the first fish were caught near the platforms, most fishermen assumed they were simply taking temporary refuge. But it developed that the presence of the rigs led to the development of ecosystems with their own resident fish. Boats from the mainland soon moored to the rigs and worked the bottoms and pilings for snapper and amberjack. Then it was discovered that the obstructions attracted schools of cobia, weakfish, and other varieties less addicted to bottom feeding.

The food chain extended out from the rigs and trolling in the general vicinity was much more productive than in open sea. The areas provided concentrations of almost any fish prevalent in the region. Charter boats concentrated on the rigs and sportsmen with small craft made the trips in convoy. Although there was frequently a concentration of pelagic fish near the wells, it was some time before anglers concluded they might actually increase the overall number of fish through their fostering of marine life. But there could be oil spills, one of the curses man has visited upon "his" oceans, and ecologists worried about future leaks. When the petroleum industry promised special care in handling offshore operations, some environmentalists wavered in their convictions. A twentieth-century cry for energy established offshore drilling permanently and more of it was promised. More of it is sure to come.

THE SURFMEN

Surf-fishing, especially that of the Northeast Coast, changed greatly with the available tackle and with the added mobility of anglers, who developed a variety of strange vehicles for beach travel. Competitive surf-casting was very popular early in the game, and some casters were throwing four hundred and fifty feet shortly after World War I. By the nineteen-thirties there were excellent reels made for the task, and some of them stayed, with modest changes, into the seventies. Van Heilner (born 1899) was an exponent of surf-fishing with its special rapport between man and the sea, and although he fished the world in deepwater boats it remained his first love. Heilner, born to wealth, became a successful author on salt-water angling and an undisputed authority on surf-fishing. His cruiser, the *Nepenthe,* was built to last and under other ownership it still serves sportsmen in Florida's Ten Thousand Islands and the Shark River country.

Heilner preached the qualities of the channel bass. The great triumvirate of the East Coast surf are the channel bass, the striped bass, and the bluefish, and it was primarily those which brought about the beach buggy, a lumbering, soft-tired marvel of the sands, built from strange discarded parts and equipped with facilities for day and night existence, if not for comfort.

The beach buggy began its reign after World War II and enabled a hardy breed of surf-casters to follow fish and rumors of fish along hundreds of miles of coast. Factory-built trucks, carryalls and campers with four-wheel drive began to replace it in a few years, but there were some fishermen who still insisted on their own creations.

The true surf-caster acquired special skills in handling his equipment and a special fund of knowledge regarding sea, beach formations, and weather. He learned to read the waves for details of the ever-changing shore contours, and threw his baits

and lures into spots that held feeding fish, but attracted no attention from novices. He practiced his sport day and night when the surf ran tall, and when it was mild he learned to launch light boats from shore to reach fish that were too far out, even for his powerful rod. These craft filled a gap between the shore fishermen and the larger salt-water bass boat, an open craft that could maneuver close to the breakers.

For the most part, the little boats rode atop beach buggies and could be lifted easily by two men. They were used with outboard motors of moderate size—powerful enough to leave the beach promptly and light enough to be manhandled quickly. Launchings became precise drills of split-second timing. The fishermen watched the seas and gauged their height, then launched their boat at the proper time, usually with one man on the oars while the other pushed off and started the motor. Boats were swamped and smashed, equipment was lost and the sea claimed some lives, but the surfman stayed, an individual proud of his sport and the things he knew about the sea. When fish were running he might be red-eyed and unkempt, but he wore his foul-weather gear with a flair.

Coastal anglers had their own national publication, *Salt Water Sportsman,* with Hal Lyman as publisher and Frank Woolner as editor. It had begun under other management in 1939 as a news sheet; with the end of the war it told the story of the beach angler while covering other salt-water activities as well.

Before World War II the tin squid was the principal artificial of the surfman. It was a simple design, heavy enough for good casting, and the tin had a glow of its own. Some fishermen felt it was superior to the chrome of a later day. Probably the first artificial plugs used in the surf had been designed for large fresh-water fish, such as muskellunge and pike, and when there was increased demand for them they were made in materials that would resist rust and corrosion. Then there was a rush of small metal lures that took bluefish and mackerel especially, but worked on other surf fish as well.

Striped bass were a success on the Pacific Coast from Oregon to southern California, and although they were caught from the surf at times the nature of the coastline was less favorable for organized invasion by beach buggies. Private ownership of beach areas brought the beach buggies into disfavor in many areas on both coasts and their owners formed self-policing associations, their effectiveness sometimes reduced by the activities of rebel beach runners, usually not interested in fishing.

Sport fishing for Pacific salmon was largely an outgrowth of the commercial fishery. Many offshore boats trolled commercially, and when there was interest in sport angling, some of their captains accepted paying clients for the thrill of hooking giant chinooks in deep water. The coho or silver was often caught by surface trolling, and all kinds of salmon were fished from small boats as they entered river mouths on their migrations.

THE CHERRY BOBBER

The steelhead was known as the salmon trout at first and members of the Lewis and Clark expedition caught them with the rods and reels they took to the mouth of the Columbia. They were the premier game fish of the Pacific Northwest, for they retained their vigor and firm flesh throughout their spawning journey, while the salmon deteriorated rapidly after entering the rivers.

Unlike the Atlantic salmon, the steelhead did some feeding after leaving the sea and they sometimes spent long periods in fresh water after they matured.

Steelhead were sometimes vulnerable to flies and streamers near the surface, and many were caught on spoons and other artificial lures but the most effective method, especially when the rivers were high, was a delicate form of bottom-fishing with highly specialized tackle. Steelhead, like most other trout, consume salmon eggs, and most salmon streams are also steelhead streams. A variety of rigs for salmon egging were devised, some of them enclosing quantities of salmon spawn in small transparent bags that allowed some of the egg's odor to drift downstream. This was followed by lures built to imitate clusters of eggs, artificial lures being encouraged when salmon eggs were declared illegal as bait in many areas. The Cherry Bobber was a pioneer of the method, beginning a unique form of angling.

Most of the early bobber fishermen employed rather long casting rods with bait-casting reels of the black-bass type, although spinning tackle served as well. The rods had sensitive tips that indicated the downstream progress of the lure as it was bounced along the bottom, and were highly efficient in casting fairly light weights. Once the system was adopted, thoughtful fishermen refined it to a meticulous technique.

The fisherman surveys the steelhead river to find heavy current that will carry his lure, and he casts out and across with slender monofilament line. The bobber goes down promptly, pulled by a pencil-shaped sinker, and is suspended just above the bottom, one end of the sinker barely contacting the gravel. The push of current causes it to go downstream slowly, the sinker end tapping gently on the way, and the fisherman watches his tip attentively. His lure is moving too slowly, he decides, so he cuts a little lead from the sinker and tries again, allowing the lure to go well below him before he retrieves it and casts once more. When his rig works exactly right he moves very slowly downstream at intervals, rod high, the tip carrying news of the sinker's progress to his trained hands.

At first the lures were nearly always colored to represent salmon eggs, but it was found later that other colors worked as well or better at times. It is the unique action just above the bottom that does the work, even when water is murky.

Steelhead are different fish in different waters, but the bobbing bottom lure was a key to other methods that worked on fish that ignored near-surface flies. It was the tournament fly casters who made bottom-fishing practical for the fly-fisherman.

Competitive casters found that by splicing light monofilament line to short sections of heavy fly line they could make much longer casts and cross the wide, heavy current the steelhead travels. Then they applied fast-sinking fly line to the task and brought their flies to the bottom, where they worked downstream much as the caster's lures did. It was the sinking "head" and monofilament running line that made steelhead fishermen of competitive casters, and the same equipment worked on salmon willing to feed a little as they undertook their upstream journey. The fly-fishermen of the Pacific Coast produced their own famous anglers, like Bill Schaadt and Myron Gregory, perhaps twenty of them, and then came more masters, most of them specialists on their own preferred rivers. Their cult was much like that of the Atlantic surf-casters.

8.

Make It A Game

Fishermen always have tried to measure their accomplishments, and although their pastime is often considered a contemplative one it cannot escape the prod of competition. The fisherman competes with the fish, seeks to outdo his past performances, and feels the urge to compare his efforts with those of other fishermen.

His success is measured in many ways. Edward Hewitt aptly described the evolution of a master angler when he said that he first wanted to catch the most fish possible, then the largest fish, and then the most difficult fish. There are fishermen who aspire to superiority in the mechanics of their game, wishing to cast farther or more accurately than others. Many have competed in the development of more efficient tackle. Although most competition-bred equipment cannot remain secret for long, each refinement usually has its brief moment of triumph in the hands of the originator.

The most common field of competition is in the size of the fish caught. A very large fish of any kind is recognized and acknowledged even by casual fishermen and the public. There is the self-imposed handicap of lighter tackle, which finally led to well-established classifications, each of which produced its own records. (Generally, the lighter the tackle the greater the achievement.) There is the classification of method, which places a premium on a fish caught on a fly, as opposed to one caught trolling or with natural bait, and the geographical division, which recognizes that a large fish from one area is a more worthy catch than one taken where such fish are relatively common.

There are overtones of commercialism that began in America when builders of rods and reels competed in casting tournaments and advertised their successes, each builder being represented by professional casters. Late in the nineteenth century a casting tournament was a part of many tackle exhibits, and when a certain rod was a winner its builder advertised the fact, often with sharp criticism of competing products. The professional sportfisherman is often a salesman, and any consistent winner in fishing competitions will be offered sponsorship by manufacturers. A winner of amateur casting tournaments who turns professional may not compete for purses, but his skills are a constant demonstration of how he uses the tackle provided by his sponsor. He becomes an adviser and a researcher, and possibly a designer.

Angling achievements of the distant past have been clouded by the absence of official records and by overenthusiastic descriptions. Many early accounts simply were not believed by later anglers, often with justification.

When the stand fishermen of the early striped-bass clubs were described by writers of their time, it was said they could throw live menhaden a hundred yards or more under favorable conditions. A century later, expert surf-casters, using much more efficient equipment, were unable to match such distances with any kind of live bait. They wondered if their ancestors meant "feet" instead of "yards."

It was the tournament casters who first began to keep score. There were national organizations for competition in the eighteen-eighties, and the current American Casting Association began as the National Association of Scientific Angling Clubs in 1906. A continuous record of fish sizes began with a *Field and Stream* magazine contest in 1911. Announcement of the first competition was made with the salutation, "Now tell the truth for once in your life!" Big-fish

*Opening pages: Flight of high-speed
bass boats takes off at start of day's fishing in
contemporary professional tournament.
Boats race to reach best fishing
grounds. Contestants have three days to achieve
greatest total weight of fish
and largest single fish. Membership in Bass
Anglers Sportsman Society, which
sponsors tournaments, is more than 200,000.*

reporters had a poor reputation for veracity.

"Matchmen" have fished competitively in England for more than seventy-five years and practice their sport on the Continent, as well. This fishing began in areas where trout were not available, and the small fish caught were more exciting with prizes or wagers. A National Federation of Anglers was formed in England in 1903, and the annual open competition run by the Birmingham Anglers Association sometimes attracts as many as five thousand entries. Most such events are conducted from shore, the fishermen separated into "swims" and sometimes no more than thirty feet from each other. No trout are entered, and the awards are on the basis of fish weight, the catch sometimes being made up of fingerling roach weighing half an ounce each.

International salt-water records followed much later with organization of the International Game Fish Association in 1939. Michael Lerner, a famous deepwater angler, was instrumental in its beginning. The IGFA has since broadened its influence in fields of salt-water fish conservation with representatives in sixty-five countries and territories.

Zane Grey would not have approved some of the stipulations attached to IGFA records, but they have served well for years with only minor changes. Because of the rules' simplicity, it was inevitable that some forms of angling would not get their due, but the IGFA was formed by deep-sea anglers and primarily for deep-sea anglers. Currently the IGFA has approved the use of gang hooks by casters of artificial lures, a concession to tackle that does not quite fit the pattern of conventional offshore operations. Fly-fishermen have set up their own organization, the Salt Water Fly Rodders of America.

But until the sixties most competition had been in fish size and not for money. The professional "cast-for-cash" tournaments of the Bass Anglers Sportsman Society began in 1968, and in less than ten years had a membership of more than 200,000, most of whom did not participate in the big tournaments but supported an organization they felt was important in the promotion of bass fishing.

Another form of competition which came forward in the late twentieth century was somewhat related to the first buttons awarded members of the old Catalina Tuna Club, but more sophisticated. It was a club classification of anglers as they might have been graduated through the chairs of a fraternal organization. To achieve a step toward a badge the angler had to catch a fish of a certain size with certain specified tackle, and he learned many of the requisite skills through club instruction.

Tournament casting, the test ground for a hundred years of tackle, faded in national importance as competition fishing grew. Champions of the nineteenth century had demonstrated products, proved the points of rod manufacturers, and achieved some importance, much as the great shooters of their day had become famous.

At times the competitive casters have been so specialized in their equipment that practical fishermen have said there was little connection between the "games" and real fishing, but the casters have altered their programs and only a few events require highly specialized equipment today. The accuracy events can be won with over-the-counter fly, bait, and spinning gear, and the Skish events require no alteration in commercially available tackle. Skish was developed by tournament casters who felt it would

WEIGHING THE RODS

*Caster throws for distance
in 1883 tournament of National Rod &
Reel Association in New York's
Central Park. Committee boat measures
cast against course markers.
Curlicues in line are evidence of
faulty cast. Inset: Contestants' rods
had weight limits for each
event and were checked on scale. Tackle
manufacturers sponsored
professional casters. Above: Denton
painting of largemouth bass.*

HARPER'S WEEKLY.

A
JOURNAL OF CIVILIZATION.

VOL. XXVIII.—No. 1445.
Copyright, 1884, by HARPER & BROTHERS.

NEW YORK, SATURDAY, AUGUST 30, 1884.

TEN CENTS A COPY.
$4.00 PER YEAR, IN ADVANCE.

appeal to fishermen with no interest in techniques that could not be applied directly to lake or stream.

The American Casting Association deals primarily with fresh-water tackle. Surf-casting tournaments are sponsored by coastal clubs, but have received less national recognition.

Only a small number of competitors now participate in the distance games. In distance bait-casting the expert uses handmade reels and the lines are too light for practical fishing. The distance cast is delivered with full-bodied and perfectly-timed swings and the shaft of the very light spool runs on an oil cushion which replaces the thumbing required with heavier lines and spools. The distance bait-caster uses a short section of shock line to absorb the initial force of his throw and relies on the oil to give his spool the exact restraint necessary as the thread line goes out. His tackle box is likely to carry a row of vials with oils of different weights for different atmospheric conditions, a technicality too complex for most casters. Even in distance events, however, the Skish tackle is practical for fishing, and spinning events are included.

One device from distance fly casting was transplanted directly to California's steelhead rivers and from there to trout, bass, and salt-water casting. It is the principle of light monofilament line which runs behind a short section of "shooting head," or heavy fly line, which provides the casting weight. The trout-fly distance event uses a rod that will serve for fishing, and the tournament casters developed the double haul, a system of adding speed to the cast by feeding line on the back cast and then hauling it back through the guides as the final throw is made, using the line hand for the hauling motion.

The salmon-fly distance event, using a two-handed rod, has little place in current American fishing, although two-handed fly rods are still in use in England and occasionally in Canada. In distance fly casting the light running monofilament is coiled beside the caster and tended by an assistant, or gillie. No reel is used.

Accuracy events require casts at floating rings on water. Much of their popularity was lost when the bass fisherman moved away from shore for much of his angling. For while the casters' accuracy is impressive, it is less so than that involved in striking a small pocket along a shoreline, or laying a lure or fly against a stump or lily pad.

There are international casting events as well, and teams of Americans travel abroad with little notice from the media. And although few American fishermen have even heard the champions' names, the tackle they use has gained much of its refinement through the internationalists' efforts.

Before the star drag made reel operation simpler, salt-water anglers could hardly conceive of landing a one-hundred-pound fish on rod and reel. And when the first rods were used for tarpon there were writers who said no man was strong enough to hold one that size except with a hand line. When the tarpon challenge was met by inshore anglers and large catches were frequent, if not commonplace, the rod and reel went farther to sea in the hands of a few wealthy men, and fish of more than a thousand pounds were caught. Zane Grey did it first with a blue marlin of 1,040 pounds, hooked in Tahitian waters in 1930. As yet, however, there was little organized record-keeping. Grey's fish had been mutilated by a shark after being hooked and such catches were later disqualified by the International Game Fish Association. The largest rod-

Contemporary fly-casting tournament course. Ring is target for accuracy casting. Anything inside is "perfect." Deductions are made from point score for lesser throws. This is more popular event than throwing for distance, primarily because gear is similar to that of everyday fisherman, while distance casting requires specialized equipment.

and-reel catch on record with the IGFA is a 2,664-pound white shark caught from an Australian beach by Alfred Dean in 1959. No boat was used.

Once record-keeping was established, the formal tournament was held, usually for salt-water fish, such as bluefin tuna or the various billfish. Tuna tournaments were frequently conducted with teams representing various countries and fishing in designated areas during set hours, but the most popular head-to-head contests were yet to come in America. Those were the black-bass tournaments, a product of fresh-water electronic equipment and the artificial impoundments, and from them came a new breed of professional sportfisherman who fished for purses, publicity, and sponsors.

SCIENCE AND BASS BOATS

The largemouth black bass was known only as a shallow-water fish by generations of fishermen. It was caught with bait and fly before the plug-casting rod became an instrument of skill. Thereafter the shoreline lure caster became an artist, laying his plug within scant inches of lily pads, grass, or boulders. He used a rod four to six feet long, usually of bamboo or steel, and his silk line was dried after each day's fishing. He knew fish were along the shoreline, he doubted they could be found elsewhere, and when fishing was poor he simply assumed the fish were neither hungry nor angry.

When the bass went to deep water in very hot or very cold weather, he concluded they were either dormant or refusing to feed. In chilly weather he hoped to find them at midday. In hot weather he sought them at dawn or dusk, but he searched for proper conditions rather than new areas in his chosen lakes and rivers. From the natural lakes

he carried the same outlook to hundreds of great impoundments and found them even more unreliable.

After World War II there were more black bass than ever before. New millions of them lived above the power dams, especially in the South. Electronic depthfinders flashed and clicked and drew their erratic lines on moving charts for salt-water fishermen, but fresh-water anglers saw no need for them at first. Their need really became known indirectly through some new fishing methods, and one lure in particular was the introduction to them.

Buck Perry's Spoonplug was a metal contrivance that ran deep when trolled or retrieved and so shaped that the faster it went the deeper it dove. Perry, an expert bass fisherman, said it was not so much the shape, color, or action of his lure that made it revolutionary, but the fact that it would actually gouge the bottom at depths seldom plumbed by bass fishermen. His method was heresy to most users of light tackle, for he said his lure should be attached to very heavy line and trolled at high speed. Used with a stiff rod, the Spoonplug would actually tear through grass and debris on the bottom, and it caught fish far from shore.

Perry said that only a few bass were to be found along the shoreline and that they spent most of their time on the bottom elsewhere. He admitted his method was not dainty and he told audiences of fishermen that once they found fish with his lure they could then use anything they chose—but he said his lure would find them. Some shoreline experts said that if only a few bass were found along the shore, those were the ones they wanted; shoreline fishing was the most sporting method. More deep-water fishermen, however, began using Perry's method, or others very similar. "Finding" bass became an important part of the game and the basis of tournament fishing, eventually being refined to the point of utilizing electronic aids.

There is a pattern of aging to artificial impoundments. It was discovered and observed before its import was understood, but by 1950 fisheries biologists could make accurate forecasts of a lake's bass-fishing cycle—a cycle extended indefinitely by the tournament fishermen and those who followed their lead. Newly flooded waters produced large fish populations, with individuals growing rapidly because of an abundance of food. Within three or four years there was exceptional fishing about partly submerged trees and along verdant shorelines. Then, as the lake aged, some of the new cover disappeared and silt built up at the stream mouths. Fishing deteriorated and the balance so favorable to black bass changed. The process was not exactly the same with all lakes, but generally the same endpoint was inevitably reached.

The days when a fisherman could watch charging bass dart upward through clear water from newly covered greenery to take a surface lure were ending, and thoughtful anglers began to recall things that had been covered by the aging lake. Beneath the surface were old roadbeds, bridges, culverts, hills, riverbeds, and even villages—an eerie landscape of drowned hiding places and logical feeding spots. Submerged rivers still flowed, more slowly but often in their old courses, bordered by what had once been shoreline with trees and cliffs. The fishermen studied old maps and drew new ones. The first miniature electronic fishfinders were built. They were powered by small batteries, and fishermen listened with headphones to the squeaks and murmurs of the under-

water world. They heard the motion of water through grass beds and the rushes of schools of bait-fish, and began to interpret the sounds of various species. But it was in the survey of "structures" that electronics was to be of most value to them.

When bass tournaments began in earnest, electronics became a necessity for winning contestants, and thousands of fishermen who never entered a contest studied the techniques of the masters and fished in new places.

The serious bass fisherman on the impoundment looks for "structure," a term which he originated to mean any underwater obstruction, anything from a drowned church building to a sloping point running from a high bank to a deep bottom. He hopes to establish a pattern of fish behavior, the perfect "pattern" running hour by hour from daylight until after dark. He does it with his depthfinder, his thermometer, and perhaps with instruments to check oxygen content and even water clarity.

In the early morning of a warm day he seeks shallow feeding areas, even as earlier shoreline anglers would have done. He finds a patch of vegetation near a creek mouth, near a deep channel and shaded by shoreline trees, and his bass boat stalks the spot with its murmuring electric motor while he watches the flickering record of his progress on his depthfinder. He casts far with his near-surface lure, attentive to any swirl or skipping fingerling. The bass stirs the surface as it strikes and is pulled from cover quickly lest it disturb others. It may be one of a school of fish.

There are other fish but they do not strike, although they leave wakes as they follow from the eelgrass patch, and he changes lures by simply

A large sailfish caught on light tackle. Angler has used bait-casting gear, with turning-spool reel, to throw a plug. This is a very sporting method of bringing in a substantial catch. Sailfish often are found cruising on surface, may be coaxed into striking with hookless "teasing lure."

*Two big fish subdued
with light tackle. Thirty-pound
dolphin (below) was taken
on fly rod in Gulf of Mexico, a
considerable feat because
of fish's habit of diving deep
when hooked. Marlin (right)
was caught from small
boat, and angler maneuvered
his fish without benefit of customary
fighting chair to take strain.*

using a second rod, already rigged. When he has caught his second bass the sun is full on the eelgrass patch and he senses that the fish have moved to deeper water. The temperature will be better several feet down, he thinks, and he studies a nearby shoreline for a telltale ridge sloping toward deep water but there is none. He looks at his topographic map and starts his big outboard motor for a run of several miles to where a spine slopes to an old riverbed. He moves his boat along its unseen crown, casting across as he goes. He has a strike and

instantly checks the water depth, information that may provide his entire day's fishing.

His huge tackle box holds lures that were popular before he was born, but there are others which are products of new methods and waters. There are the plastic worms in subtle shades of color that have proved successful for no reason he knows. There are "spinner baits," weighted plastic skirts with spinners suspended above them on little wire outriggers. There are fast-wriggling "fat plugs" made to imitate

the small shad that thrive in deepwater impoundments. And there are jig baits, not seen on fresh water until recent years.

The "pattern" of modern bass fishing might go from the early morning grass bed, to the established depth of midday feeding, to possibly very deep water where "striking" bass, or "jump bass," school up to attack bait on the surface. Some fishermen believe the "striking" black bass learned their trick from the white bass, a fish that came into prominence with the creation of deep impoundments. Where a similar procedure occurs on southern rivers they suspect the habit was learned from salt-water fish, though the presence of bait under the proper conditions could be reason enough for concerted attacks, charging fish driving bait to other bass. Finally, it is quite possible the fisherman who found bass feeding in the shallows in early morning will find them there in late evening, as well.

The tactics of the modern bass

*Big-league bass tournament attracts
top professionals sponsored by boat, tackle,
and outboard-motor manufacturers.
Officials check starters to see no fish are
stashed aboard. Powerful boats going
out and coming in. Contestants
file through crowd for weigh-in. Live bass
are weighed in plastic bags
to keep them wet until release.*

Largemouth bass is customary
target of tournament fishermen. Underwater
pair appears to be in ideal bass
habitat: slow-moving water with abundant
vegetation and cover. "Henshall-Van Antwerp"
black-bass reel patented in 1887 has
automatic drag which prevents backlash. Jumping
largemouth violently shakes head
in often-successful effort to throw lure.

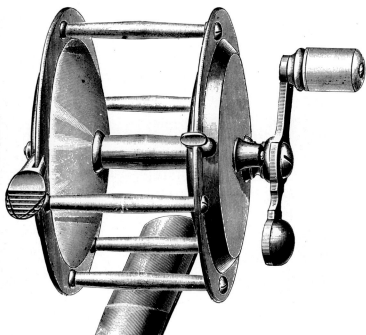

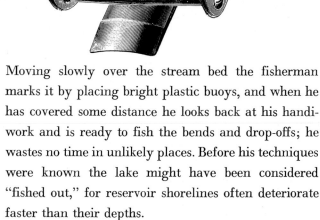

angler and his machinery are keyed to his knowledge of fish habits. He knows that although bass are commonly found near bottom, whatever the depth, there are times when they are suspended in anticipation of surface feeding, as in the case of those cruising beneath shoals of threadfin shad, or when they are near stumps or tree trunks. In the new language of the bass fisherman, emergent tree stumps have become "stick-ups." They remain in reservoirs for decades.

One of the skills of the electronic bass angler is the mapping of structures, either on paper or in his mind. He finds an underwater stream bed and visualizes it much as it was when it first disappeared from view five or fifty years ago. He knows its sharp bends mean high banks on the outside of each curve and his fathometer confirms it, even telling him what parts of the old banks are still solid or rocky and what contours have been softened by erosion or silting.

Moving slowly over the stream bed the fisherman marks it by placing bright plastic buoys, and when he has covered some distance he looks back at his handiwork and is ready to fish the bends and drop-offs; he wastes no time in unlikely places. Before his techniques were known the lake might have been considered "fished out," for reservoir shorelines often deteriorate faster than their depths.

With the new knowledge of impoundment bass came new techniques for specialized lures. The plastic worms and eels had developed a little before the bass boat, and their efficiency increased with the probing of fathometers. They were not so much precise imitations of life as an incorporation of features of eels, worms, and water snakes that bass feed on. They were generally worked slowly and hesitantly near the bottom, but resourceful fishermen also learned to fish them on the surface and through weed beds.

Roland Martin, noted professional bass
fisherman, with championship-caliber largemouth.
Equipment is all the best: electronic
fishfinder, bait-casting reel with high-speed
retrieve, swivel seat, carpeted
interior to deaden sound. "Standard American
Black Bass & Lake Flies" from catalog of
1882 are now passé. They have been supplanted
by popping bugs and streamer flies.

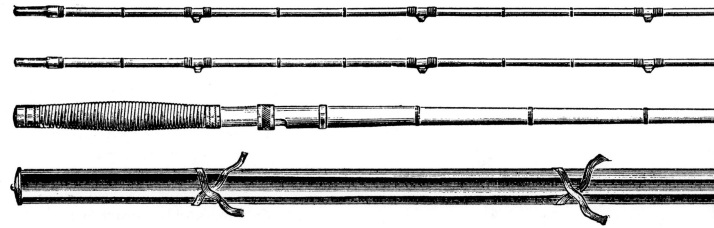

Sinking lures, such as the spinner baits, were first used in steady retrieves, but were then found to be effective when hopped on the bottom or lowered almost straight down from drop-offs. The jigs, often combined with small artificial eels, were frequently worked straight up and down at the bottom in the method popular for salt-water fish. Designers studied the sounds of lures moving through water and concluded that bass were capable of locating moving objects, even when the water was dark enough to be virtually opaque. Noisemakers were attached to some lures and the vibrations of plugs with extremely fast wriggles appeared to be transmitted for long distances underwater.

The principle of dropback was one of the important developments. Deep fishermen learned that most of their strikes came when a lure was sinking, often after a brief forward motion; whereupon lures were designed for that. The spinner bait, although effective when reeled straight, had special attraction when sinking because the spinners continued to move.

The professional bass tournament fostered a rapid development of equipment. It had a logical beginning in the South, where no other fresh-water game fish could compete with the bass, where there were many impoundments of various ages, and where the fishing season was long. Tournaments were welcomed by most resort areas, not only for the capacity crowds but for the attendant publicity. Local fishermen were interested in what the tournament experts might learn about their lake.

Substantial entry fees made tournament prizes well worthwhile, and although the tournament professional usually found it necessary to supplement his prize money with income from another job, a consistent winner found sponsors eager to supply his equipment and paint their product's name on his boat. Contestants frequently were lure, tackle, or boat manufacturers. The tournament angler dressed in colorful clothing, with patches advertising his sponsors, and might come from any walk of life. The details of an efficient operation were quickly outlined by professional promoters, and the bass tournament became an established angling event. Its champions are unknown by anglers in other fields, but carefully followed by hundreds of thousands of bass fishermen.

Most bass tournaments are now based on the overall weight of the total catch, with special awards for the largest fish. Contestants catching a legal limit of fish are permitted to cull the catch for larger ones, and many big tournaments require that the boat contain livewells, so released fish will be unharmed.

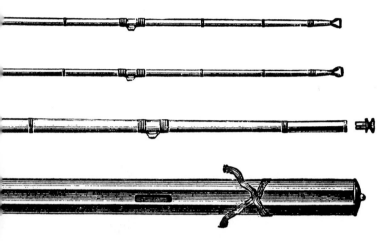

*"Little Giant" black-bass rod
was made to Dr. Henshall's specifications:
two joints, 7½ feet in length, 8½–9
ounces in weight. Designed for inland bass or
as "a light rod for sea fishing,"
it was beginning to approach the short
bait-casting rod of a later day.
Like many rods of its time, it was offered in
several materials. Below:
Three mounted largemouth bass.*

A hundred or more efficient contestants can catch a great many fish. Disposal of the catch was an immediate problem and residents of tournament lake areas feared for their bass population. At the conclusion of some contests the catch was handed over to charitable organizations, and then a release program was established. The entries were carried in livewells, then weighed and released with suitable precautions. A very large percentage of survival was reported by biologists, and one objection to the large bass tournament was surmounted.

An advanced form of competition is the blind tournament in which contestants are taken aboard a chartered airplane and flown to a secret lake where suitable boats are waiting. They are not told their destination until on board the aircraft. Thus, the fisherman is likely to be casting over strange waters, or at least waters he has not investigated lately, and must rely on his own resourcefulness for finding fish, rather than on the practice days which more conventional competitions allow.

But the mechanics of fishing contests are less important to the world of angling than the developments which come from them. The most obvious contribution is the bass boat.

It had to have considerable speed, because impoundment fishing means long-dis-

tance travel. It needed low sides to reduce wind resistance and increase fishing convenience. It had to be built long enough to accommodate two or three casters, and narrow enough so that an electric motor could pull it easily when fishing began. It required livewells for catch or bait and, generally, swivel seats. The interior is often carpeted to deaden noise and there should be an instrument panel. For steadiness when not under way, the typical boat was made with a modification of the cathedral hull. From these basic specifications the bass boat developed in all directions and became one of the most popular fishing crafts of the nineteen-seventies. It was a long way from the cypress rowboat and the pine johnboat.

Not only did the bass tournament provide a testing ground for equipment and method in expert hands, its revelations were almost instantaneous. Never before had unknown lures leaped into prominence so suddenly. It was possible for a handmade prototype to begin a day on the line of a champion and be famous before nightfall. And by the following evening several manufacturers could be preparing to tool up for their version of the new lure in a race for sales in the hundreds of thousands. No other kind of fishing has had such sudden effect on tackle manufacture and fishing method. There have been revivals of lures that had lost their popularity, and occasions when a winning lure commanded high prices while a tournament was still going on as a matter of novelty and scarcity. The Kentucky multiplying reel took some seventy years to realize its potential with appropriate rods. Such an invention could have been famous in as many minutes if it had been introduced at a bass tournament!

So the bass tournament has be-come an institution. Its entrants meet in the early morning to mop the dew from their sleek boats and powerful engines, and to speak cheerfully in carefully evasive tones. In practice sessions on the lake each contestant has sought a pattern, and if he has found a successful one he is guarded and thoughtful. If he has not, he is watchful. His success or failure may now depend on observing other fishermen.

There are two men to a boat, competing with each other as well as with other contestants. This is the policy that guarantees self-regulation and strict enforcement of rules.

The boats leave the starting line in flights. Sometimes they race, for it is possible more than one boat will be heading for the same fishing spot. Usually, they are started at intervals of a few seconds. In the larger tournaments each angler has his own livewell. Each competitor is in charge of the boat's procedure for half of the fishing period and chooses the fishing area, generally fishing from the front of the boat during the time he is in charge.

In early morning there is likely to be mist clinging to the lake's surface, and as the boats follow a bending arm of the lake their echoes change against the varying contours of the wooded shores. The boats are bright and their passengers are in life jackets, bent forward a little against the wind.

A single shoreline fisherman hurries to move his skiff away from the speeders' course and slides almost against the bank to watch their passing. As they approach from a distance, each boat is outlined against the already fading mist and their own spray, and the big engines seem first to moan and then to whine as they come closer. When they are gone the lake's narrow arm is frothed, but they have skimmed

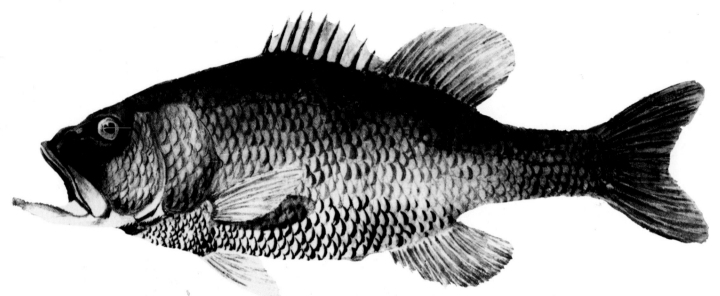

"Fish," a fairly accurate bass by Titian Ramsey Peale.

so high in the water that their wakes are slight. The shoreline angler watches from his gently bobbing skiff and hears the engines changing tune as the "flight" breaks up and begins to head its separate ways in a wider part of the lake. He remembers when there was no lake, only a river and some creeks threading through the hills. He has a vague feeling that the speeding boats do not belong there, but he begins to fish again, using a lure made famous by one of the men in one of the swift boats.

So fishermen continue to compete, and while a hundred swift bass boats line up before full daylight at some tournament locations, their gently bobbing outlines emphasized by dots of red and green running lights, there are other tourneys scarcely noticed. There are a few more boats than usual at some back-country ramp and most of their owners seem to know each other. All leave at about the same time and when they come back they compare notes with more than casual interest before moving on, their boats perched on trailers. Their small club's fishing tournament has a minimal entry fee, if any, and there is no money for prizes. If the competitor and the contemplative angler could meet on common ground they could do it best in such a setting.

It was record-keeping that made big-game fishing an international hobby; and without it knowledge of the great fishes and their migrations would have been long delayed. It was competition that developed the sporting potential of the large fresh-water impoundments, and tournament fishermen prodded piscatorial science into new areas. And even if all the fishing techniques developed by the professionals might eventually have appeared anyway, their appearance was hastened by the urgency of competition.

9. Whose Fish?

Nations and their navies have quarreled for hundreds of years over ownership of the sea's fish, the problems becoming more and more complex as food requirements and sporting values increased.

The development of commercial fishing techniques made it possible to catch more fish from a smaller stock, and exploration could not keep pace with the harvest. But the issues were clouded by fundamental ignorance of the supply. While some scientists said the sea was the future food source of the world, others argued that it had already been overexploited and that fish populations had declined as human populations increased. Another conflict emerged when sport fishing became an industry in itself. In some cases, at least, a fish was worth more at the end of a sportsman's line than in the net of a commercial fisherman. Thus there was conflict among the fishing nations and conflict between sporting interests and commercial operators. There also was conflict between the sport fishermen of one country and commercial fishermen of another, a sort of double discord.

American commercial fishermen were outdistanced in technology after World War II. It was not that other nations invented more practical fishing apparatus, but simply that the fishing enterprises of other governments were on a larger scale, a matter of national support and an urgent need for seafood. The Soviet "factory ships" were an uncomfortable factor in the cold war—floating processing plants which could serve the smaller vessels that did the actual fishing. American fliers noted that the fishing boats were equipped with complex electronic gear that was unnecessary for any kind of fishing, and the American news media called them "spy ships" in the belief they were monitoring naval and aerial activity. It was also reported that the Russian ships were equipped to track American rocket experiments.

There always had been reports that certain oceanic grounds were being fished out, but now it was being suggested that the entire salt-water population of fish could be depleted through concentrated attacks.

The Atlantic salmon situation became the outstanding example of a conflict of interests. As a sporting fish the salmon was primarily a fresh-water quarry. Commercial fishing in the upper reaches of salmon rivers had been banned for a long while. The supply had dwindled and New England salmon fishing was almost completely finished for both sporting and commercial interests by 1950. Restocking began in 1954 and there was improvement, although it was considered a token fishery. With new funds and new projects under way in the seventies the future looked better.

Americans spent a great deal of money on sport fishing for salmon in the Maritime Provinces of Canada, but until the nineteen-seventies they competed with Canadian netters. Then the Canadians decided sport fishing was more valuable than the commercial catch, and prohibited netting at the river mouths.

But many mature American salmon never came home. Adult fish roaming the deeps of the Atlantic gathered in staging areas before returning to their native streams and there they were vulnerable to the sophisticated methods of European fishermen. Not only was a large percentage of the population caught, but migrants of a particular river might be so concentrated that they could be trapped as a group a thousand miles from their spawning grounds.

Opening pages: Tournament tuna team
proudly displays 518-pounder caught off Nebraska
Shoals, between Point Judith and Block Island.
Below: Fishing for the purist—Atlantic salmon on a fly
rod, taken on St. Mary's River in
Nova Scotia. Canadian government has recognized
that income from sportsmen is greater
than from commercial catch and has prohibited
netting of salmon at river mouths.

*Age-old technique of commercial
fishermen is spreading a net supported by
floats wherever schools are running,
then hauling catch aboard. Sportsmen are not too
concerned about food fish, other than
salmon and tuna, but complain that commercial
tonnage exceeds species' ability to
replace themselves, and that
action of trawlers destroys bottom.*

It was an international quandary, a matter of one nation's fish being harvested by another in what were certainly neutral waters, and it was a problem of statesmanship at best or economic pressure at worst. The Danes, without salmon rivers of their own, were the chief offenders, taking fish from British rivers as well as those of America. When early complaints failed to change the situation, American sport anglers formed associations and announced plans for a boycott of Danish goods. Imports from Denmark exceed American exports to the country.

Finally, in the nineteen-seventies the Danes agreed to reduce their catch by stages and American salmon runs improved. It would take years to ascertain how good the agreement was, but it was a healthy sign of increasing international cooperation in fish management.

Inland fish species have long been monitored by biologists. Their scarcity or abundance can be tied to known causes, and even controlled to some extent. There is a scientific view that, given the habitat, a game fish can be nurtured and replaced if necessary. Anadromous fishes that ascend fresh-water rivers can be aided if man will forego his dams, pollution, and development. Even those species that move along the coasts can be aided and their numbers estimated to some degree, but deepwater international fish are only beginning to receive helpful attention. The concept of "driving them away" has been replaced by concern that some of the species have actually become scarce and endangered.

Bluefin tuna are no longer plentiful in most of their former haunts, and by the seventies it was evident that certain age classes had virtually disappeared. The fish caught were larger and fewer, a sign that the basic stock was not being replenished. In 1974 large fish caught north of Cape Cod were mostly over twelve years old and weighed more than five hundred pounds. Between them and youngsters of less than fourteen pounds there were very few fish, and those in small schools. The Portuguese fishery had collapsed. Then when a 1973 "class" appeared fairly plentiful, authorities termed it the "main hope for the future." It was a pessimistic view, but it was a sign that some sort of count was possible through tagging, aerial survey, and international study.

American cod fishermen of
1891 processing catch on turbulent waters off
Newfoundland. International tensions
have been intensified by
conflict between doctrine of freedom of
the seas and right of nations to
control their territorial waters. Big question
—not yet decided—is how far
off shore a nation can assert sovereignty.

Although seasons and catch limits have been relatively simple to impose on sport fishermen, they are complex when applied to the professional, especially when workers from two or more nations are involved. Government-established quotas and seasons do not touch foreign ships. Most nations with long coastlines began in the seventies to consider extending their coastal limits. Many believe a nation should control the waters as far out as the edge of its continental shelf, and a two-hundred-mile limit was suggested by American congressmen. At that point Americans would be controlling waters long considered the high seas. Canadian control extended for two hundred miles would close the Newfoundland banks to nations that had fished them for four hundred years.

There was no doubt that other nations would reciprocate immediately with extended coastal claims. Some of them had already established extended sea boundaries and impounded foreign fishing boats. The fishing grounds, often an abrasive contact point between nations, remained the scene of a cold war for protein, and the U.S. State Department was torn between détente and a fading resource.

There was no doubt that the Atlantic salmon was more valuable as a sport fish than as canned seafood, but decisions were not so simple with other fish, especially those that spent part of their lives in fresh water and part in salt. Laws aimed at conservation of the resource often posed the paradox of strictly enforced limits and seasons for the sportfisherman, while unrestricted commercial fishing continued a long cast away. Local animosities flared repeatedly.

The striped bass has been both commercial fish and sport quarry, and professionals sometimes crowded sport fishermen on the beaches, feeling a family's livelihood was more important than anyone's hobby. The surf-caster, expecting only a fish or two, found himself shouldered aside while tons of fish were rolled up in nets. His arguments were not only in defense of his sport, but in defense of the supply itself. When laws restricted inshore commercial fishing the netter felt discriminated against, especially if the sportfisherman could legally sell his catch.

Two other fish, the steelhead of the Northwest and the snook of the Southeast, were a somewhat different problem. By designating these as game fish and prohibiting their sale altogether, laws set precedents in assessing the sporting value of individual species. Both fish spend much of their lives in fresh or brackish waters.

The Florida "snook law" set bag limits as well as size limits on a fish that was of minor commercial importance, but which could be overharvested in cold weather. The snook becomes lethargic when the water cools and can be netted with equipment that would not hold it at other times. Since cold weather could not be planned, there were times when the market was glutted with snook, many of which were wasted. Loss of the snook to commercial fishermen was not so much an immediate hardship as a "foot in the door" by sporting interests. Like many other regulations, the law was oversimplified. Some kinds of snook never exceed the minimum legal length of eighteen inches, but it would have been impossible to enforce more complicated legislation.

The steelhead controversy was even more complex, for Pacific salmon and steelhead are often caught together by commercial fishermen. An Oregon law passed in 1974 prohibited the netting and sale of steelhead trout except by Indians. That was the

last of the northwestern states to protect the species.

The steelhead measure was placed on the Oregon ballot after a petition of some forty thousand signatures. It was one of the more spectacular efforts ever undertaken by sportfishermen, and both sides campaigned fiercely. Sport anglers brought in prominent speakers from other parts of the country to help spread the word that steelhead runs had faded alarmingly in the rivers of the Columbia system.

Steelhead had not been caught by commercial salmon fishermen purely by accident. When they could be sold along with the salmon catch it was possible for a fisherman to concentrate on methods and areas where steelhead would predominate in the take. Admittedly, most steelhead caught by accident would be killed, but the new law stated that such fish must be delivered to the state for distribution to public institutions or charitable organizations. Only the Indian rights to steelhead remained inviolate.

With the "steelhead laws" sports-

men won a major part of their battle against commercial interests, although there remained points of coastal friction elsewhere. A trend in the sportsman's favor had been established, and conservationists preached that commercial fishing could be liberalized in any field where a surplus developed.

A DEMOCRATIC SEA

Offshore fishing became a democratic sport in many ways. The charter boat for small parties went to deep water for billfish, for much smaller fish, such as the mackerels or bluefish, and sometimes to drift for bottom species. The small offshore craft made blue water available for family angling, while the party boat brought a day's action on the ocean to the occasional fisherman at minimal cost.

Although it goes for a variety of fish from many ports, the party boat is a growing institution, a deep-sea craft that usually makes one-day trips, sometimes leaving before dawn with the regulars occu-

Modern commercial technology is
exemplified by 800-foot, 43,000-ton Soviet
"fishing base," Vostok, which
can catch and process 300 tons of fish
per day. Right: One of 14
fishing boats carried on deck is lowered
away. Far right: Below-decks
cannery. Top right: Another Soviet fishing
fleet gathering herring (processed
by crew, below) in Sea of
Okhotsk, off Kamchatka Peninsula.

204

In simpler times, Long Island fishermen
divide a modest catch at day's
end, and broad-beamed fishing boats of 1887
tie up at landing slip for New York's
famous Fulton Fish Market.
Variety of catch made Market an ideal resource
for scientists like Louis Agassiz
to study fish species and resolve confusions
in nomenclature and identification.

pying their favorite places at the rail. From California the boat may follow schools of yellowtail with live-bait tanks and light rods. On other coasts the objectives may be snapper or grouper, and the successful head-boat captain is an expert with his bank of electronic instruments and his knowledge of wrecks, reefs, and currents. Such large party boats have brought deep-sea interests to thousands of inlanders who make only occasional trips to the coast. Offshore fish belong to them as much as to owners of sleek sportfishermen with nodding outriggers.

Artificial reefs are generally community projects and only wide public interest in fishing could have given them a beginning. Angling clubs and other sportsman's groups were first in their promotion and the first reefs generally were large ones. Old ships and barges were sunk, and followed by countless tons of wrecked cars. Then it was found that in shallow waters much smaller reefs, made of anything that could withstand current movements and hold marine growth, would attract fish. Even automobile tires, weighted with cement, could begin a submerged colony of life.

On a smaller scale the fishing reefs did what the offshore oil rigs had done. They were certain to concentrate fish and might possibly increase their numbers. Some students believe that the bottom obstacle, in addition to its attraction as a feeding station, is used by fish as a reference point in what may otherwise be a featureless expanse of water. At any rate, a large fish may be attracted to a structure so small that it affords him neither safety from larger predators nor ambush for his own feeding forays.

Floating obstacles attracted fishermen, who found moving shadows about buoys, wooden wreckage, and even vegetable crates that had drifted from the sea lanes. A giant dolphin might associate with a scrap of lumber hardly as broad as its tail. A barracuda caught from a small buoy would be replaced by another of similar size within days or hours, and other floating things might attract anything from tripletail to cobia.

Artificial reefs brought fish almost to the fisherman. Many of them could be reached with small craft unfit for long trips to sea. Then there were fishermen who began to use their own private floating reefs; there was the simple expedient of scattering newspapers to attract dolphin, and the more sophisticated construction of canvas platforms for towing behind a fishing boat, or for drifting nearby to attract wanderers—which might otherwise be attracted by a surfaced sea turtle. Or a structure of wooden slats could be suspended beneath the surface for days, held in place by a bottom anchor, its location known only to its owner.

If man does, indeed, farm the sea some day, he will have had a few garden plots to begin with.

THE ESTUARIES

The crossroads for game fish is where fresh water meets salt, a location which may change with wind and rain. The importance of these intersections dawned slowly, after homes and factories had usurped hundreds of them in a trend that could not be reversed.

On the Alaskan coast the estuary is likely to be a fiord, a precipice-bounded inlet fed by slightly creamy glacial streams coming down abruptly from forested heights, sometimes with a short beach separating the mountains from the cold depths of the Pacific with its giant halibut, its whales, and flocks of puffins.

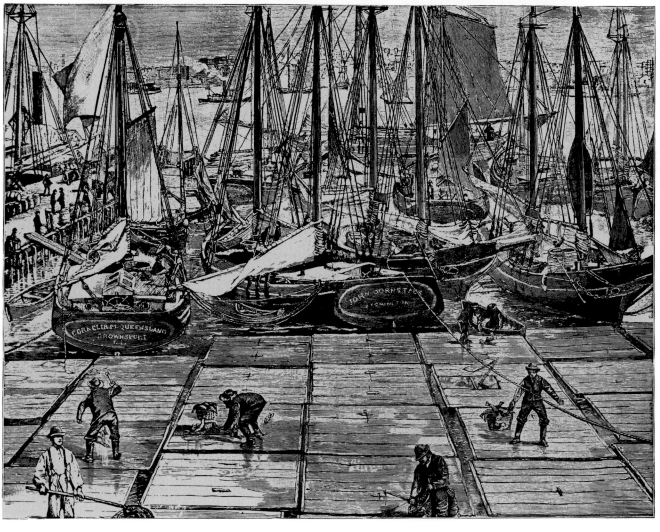

*Magnificent 696-pound bluefin tuna
is horsed aboard during 1972 International
Tuna Cup Match, off Cape St. Mary, southwestern Nova
Scotia. This splendid fish is no longer
plentiful in most of its former
haunts. Certain age classes have almost
disappeared. Those caught are
larger and fewer, an indication that basic
stock is not being replenished.*

Beneath the cliffs the runs of salmon and steelhead gather for the final lap of their journey, and airborne sea birds are moving white dots against green slopes streaked by gleaming brooks. Farther north the sea is bordered by tundra and the coastal slope is gradual.

Most of the northwestern American coast south of Alaska is rocky, but there are lagoons and strips of beach, and some of the river mouths accommodate not only the annual salmon runs but the in-and-out traffic of striped bass and bottom species. The

San Francisco Bay area has its giant marshes, similar to those of the Atlantic seaboard, pinched by the inroads of dredging and filling. There is less marsh to the south of San Francisco, and the Gulf of California brings the sea against arid and crumbling mountains. There the deepwater angler may seek yellowtail from a skiff.

The shores of eastern Canada lack the mountain heights of Alaska, but they have the forests and cold rivers. The coast of New England has rough stone and smashing tides, but at Long Island the view changes and the marshes begin to appear in broader expanses. From the Hudson River south the estuaries broaden and the marshes are wide flats. The sounds and sand islands shift their outlines as directed by the coastal storms; the vegetated marshland is more permanent. Below mid-Florida the coast changes gradually to coral reefs and mangrove swamps, part land and part water; and the Gulf of Mexico shorelines are ragged and indefinite with rivers and begin with marshland. The Everglades is a slow river of grass that forms a network of smaller streams which move with the tides. Around the entire Gulf the rivers come in broad and sluggish, their influence strung far out into the shallow Gulf, often carrying their own color with them. Where dredging has straightened and deepened them they are hampered in their historical role, and earthen canal banks have eroded with the wash of tide and boat wakes. The fresh water is mixed too quickly with salt, its contribution lessened in the process.

The drab salt marsh is the most fertile of wetlands, more fertile than the gleaming trout stream, more fertile than the tidal rivers, the depths of the continental shelf, or even the midwestern farmland. It is an essential beginning of food chains that extend far to sea, where their users know only the depths and have never cruised the coastline.

The estuary that divides the marsh is traveled by anadromous fish that ascend it to spawn and then return to the sea, but there are other fishes that perform the process in reverse. There are fishes that reproduce at sea and send their young to the rivers for development, young that sometimes drift with tidal movements and without conscious design.

The striped bass spawns in fresh water, although generally the tribe spends most of its life in brackish or salt water. When a rising tide carries small coastal foragers to the fruitful edges of the marshes to feed upon the tiny things that teem among the grasses there are striped bass that follow them, and the fisherman hooks the larger predator far from the sea.

The red drum or channel bass spawns along the open beaches, while its young invade the inshore waters, as do those of tarpon of the southern coasts, and when tiny specimens were found well inland in fresh-water puddles it was first believed their parents had somehow worked their way to fresh water to spawn.

Fishing methods of the bays and estuaries borrow from river and inland lake. The spotted weakfish, or sea trout, lives its span in and near the salt marshes and tidal rivers. It depends on the protection of the vegetation of brackish waters and feeds on the variety of life that comes from it.

In summer heat the "trout" is active at dawn and evening on southern flats that are separated from the surf by a border of beach, generally somewhat away from the quickly moving water of the navigated inlets. In colder weather it will move to deep pockets or the channels that have been gouged to accommodate inland boat traffic.

The fisherman leaves at dawn, and it is likely the lights at the dock will be hazed by insects. The morning flights of birds are pink in the sunrise, the herons going alone or in pairs, the white ibis and egrets in steadily beating lines, and by the time the fisherman reaches his chosen bar its shallowest crown is marked by the wading birds.

He anchors his boat in a foot of water and then wades a little deeper to cast his lure across light-colored sandy patches and across other bottom that is dark with grass. He knows the red drum

*Party boats do not provide the most
elegant fishing, but smart skippers usually
know where the fish are, and
it's hard not to catch something. Artist A.B. Frost has
some fun with a turn-of-the-century
day on choppy water. Two contemporary boats
land groupers large and small
(opposite), while handliners of 1880 (right)
hurl squid into breakers for bluefish.*

6.

9.

or channel bass may be moving in the shallows at this time, but he is especially watchful for the swirls made by schools of spotted weakfish, and there may be shrimp or small bait-fish leaping clear of the surface.

The trout strikes loudly at the surface plug. The wader has found a school of small ones, but he leaves them to move cautiously along the bar for a chance at bigger fish, which are more likely to be feeding alone. He sees porpoises in slightly deeper water, visitors that have entered the Inland Waterway through an inlet a few miles away, and a variety of small fish stirs little mud boils as they dart away from his carefully placed feet. He scuffs his canvas shoes along the bottom so there will be no chance of stepping on a sting ray, and is momentarily deceived by a school of mullet that makes trout-like disturbances well ahead.

When the sun has been up for two hours, the fisherman gets his boat and moves to deeper pockets where he may find trout or channel bass avoiding the midday heat. If he has no luck there he can move to the inlet, where water goes swiftly much of the day. There the ocean travelers may linger to meet the food that comes from the salt marsh and the fertile inland lagoons. There may be raiding bluefish or a concentration of pompano, and cobia could be about the jetties. He is at the crossroads and is a fishing opportunist. In the tossing waves just outside the inlet other boats troll for king mackerel, and if it is a very quiet day he may leave the inlet in his skiff, working near the shrimp boats that patrol a little offshore. On other days he has fished immediately behind them where tarpon waited for refuse fish discarded from the nets. On some days the silver giants will enter the inlet itself. Even the roving bonito may come "inside" at times in search of food.

*Handsome striped bass (left)
caught by surf-caster on New Jersey shore. Until
passage of laws restricting inshore fishing,
commercial fishermen and sportsmen
competed for stripers. Snook (below) caught in
Florida estuary is of less commercial
importance, but was overharvested
in cold weather, thus glutting market and
wasting fish—until protected by legislation.*

MULTIPURPOSE FISH

Many brackish-water species are capable of prosperity in completely fresh water for varying periods, but most of them require sojourns in salt water to complete their life cycles.

The striped bass was known to be a fresh-water spawner but a completely new facet of that prized inshore species was discovered about 1948. It could live and reproduce entirely in fresh water. Possibly other striped bass had lived their lives without the salt, but it was the Santee-Cooper Reservoir of South Carolina that proved it could be done. When the Santee and Cooper Rivers were dammed for hydroelectric power, it was assumed that striped bass trapped above the dam would live out their lives and disappear, but in a few years there were smaller fish to be caught with the older specimens and the conclusion was unquestionable. They had established full-time fresh-water residence.

The striper had a reputation of tolerance for other species. It had lived with largemouth bass and a variety of panfish in many bays and estuaries. In the Santee-Cooper Reservoir it was an addition rather than a substitution. Few inland waters could provide the exact conditions necessary for spawning, but it was learned that artificially spawned fish could be a success in lakes where a new game fish was needed. State and Federal hatcheries began to supply the "rockfish" for inland waters all over America, and in many cases they helped to solve a rough-fish problem that had arisen with the natural aging of lakes. They loved the teeming threadfin shad. Some fifteen states now have striped-bass populations in catchable quantities in their landlocked waters.

There had been a successful

212

Tops in sport fishing for many
anglers is playing a big tarpon on
light tackle. Yet much of the work can be
avoided and—depending on your point
of view—much of the sportsmanship compromised
by use of light airplane to locate fish.
Tarpon particularly show clearly
against light-bottomed flats, but planes also are
used for blues, stripers, channel bass.

striped-bass hatchery on the Roanoke River of North Carolina before 1900. Now the fresh-water possibilities seemed endless. Most of the reservoirs accommodating the new residents were in the South and the invasion seemed restricted only by water temperature, the striper demanding cooler habitat than some shallow lakes could provide.

Then in the seventies it was found that a hybrid involving the rockfish and the closely related but smaller and less respected fresh-water white bass was feasible. The resultant fish grew much larger than the white bass, but retained much of its tolerance for warm water. Even in Florida there were introductions to shallow lakes that would not have suited the striper. By 1974 there had been successful two-way crosses, involving males and females of both species. It was not known whether there might be reproduction from the hybrids, but that was a minor shortcoming. Hatchery procedure had advanced to the point where large quantities of fingerlings or sub-adults could be produced. Fishing methods for the new fish lagged behind the research, but sport anglers began to work earnestly on their new quarry.

Thermal pollution, a result of industrial plants that warmed fresh water excessively, led to still another experiment that bore fruit in 1974. The snook had demonstrated an ability to live and fight in completely fresh water, sometimes a hundred miles from the ocean, but artificial propagation had not been accomplished until 1974.

Because of its restricted American range and minor commercial value there had been little study of the snook. It had been declared a game fish and all commercial fishing had become illegal. Even its spawning habits were disputed until biologists ob-

American shad is another species shared
by commercial netters and sportsmen.
Since migrations are easily predicted, netting,
such as that by old-time Florida crew
(right), can devastate a river
for angler like modern caster (bottom). Wise management
protects spawners while permitting
reasonable commercial harvest. Below: Angler
removes plug from good-sized snook.

served the milling antics of large gravid fish in Florida passes among mangrove islands. It was the same process as that of other fish which release their spawn without nest building. They reproduced during the warm months.

Utilizing sport-fishing methods, Florida Game and Fresh Water Fish Commission biologists collected their spawners in passes on the Gulf Coast with tank trucks, tank boats, and other apparatus standing by. During the highest tides of the summer they waded at night to cast lures and flies into humid darkness and to feel the slow takes and heavy tugs of large unseen fish that had entered the passes for the spawning ritual. Although there were snook to be caught elsewhere, it was in such "controlled" conditions with screeching reels, humming insects, and rainstorms that they caught the individuals nearest to their spawning time. There were heartbreaking handling losses of captured fish and the mistakes attendant upon all such new enterprises were made, but finally they looked through the glass wall of their laboratory tank and saw tiny snook. The fish might never reproduce in landlocked fresh water but the supply could be assured. Compared to the workaday success of fresh-water trout hatcheries such triumphs were little noted by sport fishermen, but they changed the horizons of fish culture.

While the values of commercial versus sport fishing were easily calculated for some fish, others were questionable and the man with nets competed directly with those using rods. The American shad is such a fish. Its migrations are easily predicted and netting can be deadly in the rivers where casters and trollers fish for pleasure. Management, which has been successful for a century, involves allowing a sufficient number of spawning fish to go upstream while still permitting a controlled harvest for the market.

The shad is a mystery at sea, but its upstream migrations are noted by its gentle rolls, or "washes," as it comes inland each year. On some of the southern rivers of the East Coast the runs are as early as December or January. Florida's St. Johns River is the southernmost shad fishery of importance and most of that sport fishing is by trolling tiny jigs, or "shad darts," and miniature spoons, although the caster with a spinning or fly rod can make his mark if he finds a spawning area.

The little lures are trolled just above the bottom. Outboard motors idle, the boats sometimes moving in slow parades to the irritation of speedboaters and those aboard larger craft. When the best area is passed the fisherman turns and goes back over his chosen bottom as part of an endless procession. The fish takes with a plucking strike and runs wildly against a light drag to jump and earn his name as the "poor man's tarpon." Finally he is a darting target for the landing net, the little lure lodged precariously in his papery mouth, and a new rush may begin after the angler thinks he has won.

Farther north, on both the Atlantic and Pacific Coasts, the shad is caught mainly by fly tackle. The northern fish run larger, with more survival after their first spawning trip. The shad is a democratic fish but can be particular about lures and presentation, and the gleaming shad flies of one day may be inferior to more subdued designs on the next. In some rivers the fishing method is much like that for steelhead, even to fly patterns. When the catch comes easily it is hard for modern anglers to believe that there have been times when shad were considered something special, and preferable to a glut of Atlantic salmon.

*Following pages: Joe Brooks fishing for
brown and rainbow trout on western
spring creek. This is precise and delicate fishing
in American waters most
like English chalk streams. Since they are
spring-fed and do not depend on
rain run-off, these streams enjoy a
consistent flow and well-established and
predictable insect hatches.*

WHAT'S FAIR?

The light airplane that has brought hidden wilderness lakes within short hours of great cities has become a questionable tool of both sport and commercial fishermen. It has shown the schools of giant tuna as dark torpedoes, and when the king mackerel are on the surface its radio has sent fishermen to the spot within minutes.

When moving schools of big tarpon approach the light-bottomed flats the airplane can find them quickly, and the flier sometimes hurries from the airstrip to his waiting skiff, the hardest part of his search already accomplished. The plane has worked for bluefish, stripers, and channel bass, often with watchers afloat looking for a telltale dip of wings or a brief dive at the target area.

The aircraft finds and pinpoints the streaks of sargassum weed, where dolphin move in schools, or as pairs of large fish, and sometimes it finds the fish themselves or the shoals of bait they follow. It can find the swarming sea birds in their swinging funnels and join them in their betrayal of feeding game fish.

Sometimes the aircraft's role is bizarre. Near an inlet in the Southeast, for instance, a fisherman stares downward from his chartered plane, looking for the angular dark patches of giant manta rays that are feeding off shallow beaches. They move slowly near the surface, sometimes breaking water in crashing somersaults, a ton of outlandish creature high above the waves. When the fisherman has found the devilfish he goes back to shore, returning with his boat. He approaches a giant slowly. Occasionally he misjudges and is startled to find the water suddenly black beneath him. He is traversing the great fish itself.

But it is not the manta he wishes to hook. Within casting distance of it, he throws his lure at the eerie shadow's edge and waits for a rush of smaller shadows: cobia charging from beneath their living roof. The ray sounds or hurries off, and the angler is left with a singing reel and a stubborn fish that first tries to stay with the ray and then wages battle alone. At other times the cobia may follow sea turtles or flotsam.

Since sport fishing is a matter of deliberate handicaps imposed by the angler himself, there have been claims that the spotting aircraft is an unfair advantage, but the circumstances have varied too much for established rules.

QUALITY OR QUANTITY?

Fresh-water trout can be wild or "tame" and appear in many stages between. Science has learned the manner of their propagation, and the fingerlings that were depended upon in early plantings have been replaced for the most part by fish of catchable size. Only with proper habitat is the wild trout secure, but the put-and-take philosophy is scorned by many accomplished fishermen in conflict with promoters of tourism. In the trout's case, especially that of the rainbow, it is a question of whether there shall be fish for the casual angler or fish for the devoted expert, and sometimes it appears that there is not room for both.

In some healthy trout streams, naïve hatchery fish have been added as a surplus commodity for easy catching. Near a bridge on a western river the veteran fly-fisherman judges the water carefully and recognizes a perfect stretch for his work, not too swift and easily approached. He chooses his fly and lays it neatly at the head of the run, a flow bulging a

little over hidden boulders with only a few bubbles from upstream rapids. The fish takes instantly, a rainbow a foot long, and the angler smiles with satisfaction, for he has planned a long time and traveled a long way. When his first fish is released he casts again and another fish comes hard and jumps splashily. With the third or fourth catch he examines his trout carefully and notices its rather drab color, the broken areas among its scales, and the slightly frayed tail, worn from the crowded confines of a hatchery pool. A fin has been trimmed by a hatchery worker; he sees the tracks of a tank truck on a nearby bank and he leaves for another area. Much of the fun has gone out of his conquests.

The hatchery fish have been there for only a few days and they have moved very little, schooling in easy water that best matches their hatchery home. A beginning trout fisherman can find them and catch his limit, and he may have come there because he knows the hatchery truck's schedule. In some planted waters the new fish may choose strange foods in preference to the winged insects, fresh-water shrimp, or nymphs sought by his wild ancestors. The planted trout may take bits of liver, grains of canned corn, or bits of cheese, but to the casual fishermen it may be a worthy catch.

At first many hatchery fish were simply an added attraction to the already well-populated water of warier residents, and the only dispute between serious anglers and put-and-take advocates concerned the money spent. It was better applied to habitat improvement or preservation, the wild-trout lovers said. When it was found that under most circumstances planted trout soon disappeared whether caught or not, the waste was emphasized. Finally, there was a completely new concept. Electrical shocking ap-paratus became an accurate tool of census and examination. Fish could be immobilized temporarily, counted, examined, and returned to the water unharmed. It was used to study the welfare of both planted fish and wild residents, and to the surprise of biologists it was found that an influx of hatchery fish in an area not only did not increase the overall population, but soon tended to reduce the numbers of resident trout. It was believed they were displaced by the newcomers, left their established territories, and simply disappeared. At any rate they could not be found.

The wild trout were stronger and more efficient foragers than the invaders, but perhaps the density of population simply worked against nature. Conservation agencies concluded that planted fish were worthwhile only where there was insufficient native population, and many of them felt a population would seek its own level under reasonable fishing pressure.

Fishing stress could be regulated several ways. Closed seasons and small limits accomplished part of the purpose, and restrictions on baits and lures went somewhat farther. There were waters closed to natural baits, others that were open to fly-fishing only, and finally came the catch-and-release concept, with fishermen allowed to keep trophy fish or no fish at all.

Responses were almost instantaneous where fish had to be returned. Waters so regulated lost most of their fishermen to the delight of the master angler, a fellow who rarely kept his trout anyway. It was a move toward what had come to be known as "quality trout water," but it was repugnant to those who felt trout-fishing was for the masses and that the skillet was as important as aesthetic values. So trout became a political question, especially in western states

"Ouananiche Fishing," watercolor by Winslow Homer.

that still had numerous wild-trout streams.

Serious trout fishermen took heart with policy changes in Yellowstone National Park, an area likely to be an ultimate stand of quality trout water. The millions of tourists who viewed the park's natural wonders traditionally gathered for easy trout fishing, many of them never fishing in their home states. Fishing Bridge became a tourist landmark comparable to Old Faithful and Mount Rushmore.

Fishing Bridge spanned the Yellowstone River and native cutthroat trout passed under it on their summer spawning runs. Tourist fishermen stood elbow to elbow against its rails and lowered bait to the vulnerable trout, hoisting them by the thousands. The fishermen who caught them were not experts and most of them had hardly heard of releasing fish. So the cutthroats were put on strings and photographed, then taken to campers, tents, and cottages. The following day many of them appeared again, this time in the park trash cans, and the garbage collectors

Spear fisherman—here capturing a good-sized grouper—represents the new breed of underwater sportsmen. Divers' appearance in favorite waters of hook-and-line anglers, and boatloads of fish their tournaments produced, brought groups into conflict at first. But spear fishermen have controlled their activities admirably, and there now is room for everyone.

could take a creel census of their own.

The bridge was a drain on the resource, but there was hesitancy about discontinuing it, for it had become an institution. However, the park authorities *did* discontinue it and conservationists waited for the outcries. They did not come. A public beginning to accept the teachings of ecologists accepted the Fishing Bridge as a means of studying the trout's life-style.

Long sections of the park's streams have been closed to fishing and nowhere are there large limits. Flies-only regulations have thinned the ranks of fishermen in many places, and only serious anglers seem to visit the streams where all fish must be released. It was a victory of quality fishing for the few over meat-fishing by the many, and although the principle may not apply to other angling it is essential for the dwindling streams that support wild trout.

Yellowstone Park is the controlled situation on a large scale, its managers unhampered by private ownership, irrigation, damming, or industrial pollution, and they asserted themselves firmly. For many years brown trout, rainbow trout, and grayling have been present, although the cutthroat is the only native salmonid. New policies do not include the nurture of fish other than those found when the first explorers gaped at Yellowstone's roaring geysers and boiling mud pots. So although the others will not be removed, the cutthroat will receive preference, and if the others can hold their place they can enhance the fishery for those who consider the introduced fish in some ways superior.

Now the dedicated trout seeker can wade alone in many park streams, while the tourist thousands pass on nearby roads. He fishes in an instant wilderness, his efforts watched by Canada geese, blasé bison, and mildly curious elk. The coyotes hurry only a little way from his path and moose are in no rush to leave the water ahead of him. Sometimes he can see and be seen by mountain sheep, and although the animals may not be completely wild, neither are they tame. He walks only a short distance along the stream before the path fades and there may be no human footprints at all. If his wilderness is partly contrived, it is not completely so.

Other quality trout angling is reduced, however, not only by demands upon land and water but by angling pressure, and it has suddenly become measured in cash as well as aesthetic value. Paid fishing has long been the rule on salmon streams of America and Europe through private or club leasing and ownership. Now proprietors of trout water, where previously not even permission was necessary, are suddenly aware that fishing privileges have value, like crops and livestock.

The most expensive trout waters of all are those of spring-fed creeks that maintain constant flows and regular hatches of insects. In a few cases conservation groups have actually paid owners for public fishing in such places, but the cost is too great. The public is faced with the alternatives of paying individually or going to places where the fishing is less technical, however good. Access is becoming the problem of the growing numbers of trout fishermen in many areas, and where access is easy the pressure grows beyond toleration. The put-and-take process is a partial solution and catch-and-release is no longer a novelty. In many eastern streams the principal opening-day problem can be finding room to stand for hatchery fish rather than a long stretch of unoccupied stream.

The catch-out pond is a solution for anglers concerned with taking fish by simple means, a managed pool with the fish bought and paid for as they are caught—fish raised in private hatcheries that also provide trout for restaurants. It works not only for trout but for panfish and catfish in appropriate settings. In its own way the catch-out pool is comparable to the shooting preserve, where the city hunter can buy his game in settings that vary from nearly wild to those of the game farm. And if such sport lacks the flavor of the wilderness, it does draw those who might otherwise add to the congestion in more remote surroundings.

Fish farming for direct sale can be closely related to the catch-out pond, but the fisherman who pays for his catch may show the operator more profit than he could derive from the fish themselves. In some fish farming there is a diminishing return when the protein used in fish food equals that produced by the final product. Fresh-water fish farming is a complex business. The farm pond managed for personal recreation is a growing resource.

HAND TO FIN

Only in recent years has man equipped himself for underwater sport fishing. The wet suit, scuba equipment, and a new interest in the underwater world produced spearfishermen whose skills became too polished in some areas.

The diver, despite his daring and expertise, found himself at odds with hook-and-line anglers in many locations, especially those where casters were chagrined at the spectacle of a masked creature with swim fins and a spear in what had been considered a fruitful spot. There were some conditions in which the contact became argumentative and even violent. It was true that certain concentrations could be depleted quickly by those who "shot" fish and spearfishing came under many legal controls shortly after it became popular following World War II.

The spearfishing tournament was especially irritating to salt-water rod users who deplored boatloads of fish weighed for prizes, even though the fish were used for food or sold in a legal market. Later the spearfishermen began to police their own ranks stringently. The real surprise had been that many fish species were so tolerant of a man in their element. Their instincts had not been programmed for such a unique enemy.

But mutual respect solved the angler-diver problem in many areas, and with suitable restrictions the divers went their way. Their contributions to marine science have been tremendous and few fishery studies are now conducted without the observations of expert divers. In time it was realized the diver was not necessarily a raider with a bloody spear.

UNWANTED CROPS

Of all the problems afflicting modern fish management none is more delicate than that of vegetation. The balance becomes more acute as pollution destroys some needed plant life and encourages other growth.

A southern fisherman finds his bass and panfish plentiful along banks of hydrilla, for they have food and shelter there, but then the plant increases and usurps the avenue he has followed with his boat and his fishing is ended. He catches fish among floating water hyacinths and then they cover his river, and when they freeze or he sprays them with chemicals they die, sink to the bottom, and become a sludge that destroys the natural bottom habitat. Dormant plants

return when conditions are favorable and the process begins again.

When water becomes overfertile it can choke on a variety of weeds. Without cover a lake may seem sterile, but when growth appears it may go too far. The practice of the drawdown has improved fishing in many overfertile impoundments, exposing broad flats to healing sunlight. When the lake is filled again the fishing is better, for a time anyway. Along the shorelines of natural bodies of water the water depth and coverage vary constantly, and artificial fluctuations have copied nature.

Chary of repeating a mistake made with another carp of another century, fish managers in southern waters have worked cautiously with the white amur, a giant grass carp of the Old World, a vegetarian addicted to many of the harmful plants of fresh water. Sometimes reaching a hundred pounds, the fish appeared harmless at first but enthusiasm and caution have caused lawsuits and political stirrings. So far, it has proved helpful in some locations and is a guarded experiment in others.

ORGANIZED AID

Hundreds of fishing and general conservation organizations have been the backbone of fish study, protection, and propagation. Their numbers grow, and some of them appear as temporary alliances for specific projects. Trout Unlimited, organized in Michigan in 1959, is dedicated to the improvement of trout-fishing. It is a truly national organization and its chapters have led drives against a variety of trout-stream hazards. In one instance, Trout Unlimited even raised funds to lease water for the public, and it holds a special niche in conservation because trout streams can be destroyed

very quickly through industrial practices. Only prompt recognition of problems by specialized observers can prevent catastrophe.

The Sports Fishing Institute was formed in 1949 by manufacturers of tackle and associated products for fishermen. A large part of the institute's funds is used in university research, fellowships, and the conservation of fisheries through publicity. It relates to all kinds of sport fishing.

The Dingell-Johnson Law that passed Congress in 1950 was a triumph for sport fishing. It showed the fisherman's willingness to pay his own way and it provided a permanent source of funds for projects beneficial to angling. Supported earnestly by angling groups, it placed a ten percent excise tax on sport-fishing equipment, the funds issued through the Bureau of Sport Fishing and Wildlife to states and territories for fishery projects.

When management or research project is approved, Dingell-Johnson funds make up seventy-five percent of its cost, the state paying the rest. Since most of the state's share comes from license fees, such work is truly paid for by the anglers themselves.

In the seventies there was a new kind of research and management unit, completely funded by private monies, and although some ecologists scorned it as a public-relations scheme, it made progress. It was the ecology laboratory set up by coastal developers who were changing the natural scene with their building. Its purpose was to minimize damage to a fishery, or to improve it beyond its former status. Even the most ardent opponents of the developments were forced to admit that the developers were trying to "clean up after themselves."

10. Greenheart

to Graphite

Spinning tackle revolutionized American fishing immediately after World War II. Until then tackle development had proceeded slowly, if logically, from the multiplying reel and the split-bamboo rod.

Spinning was a method for the multitudes, a sporting method for the occasional fisherman who lacked the time or motivation for practice with bait-casting or fly-fishing tackle. Although the expert spinfisherman might have as much technical knowledge and skill as any dry-fly angler, it was possible for the beginner to learn to cast within a few minutes. To the casual angler, bait casting and fly casting were mysterious skills and simply too much trouble. Spinning initiated millions of new fishermen. They crowded fishing waters to the displeasure of veteran anglers, but they bolstered the ranks of those who supported fish-conservation measures.

Spinning was a long time reaching America. In fact, the principles of spinning had been used in Europe even before the Kentucky multiplying reel was thought of. It was a matter of coiling a line about some object and throwing the bait so the line would come off in loops. The process has been called "frame casting," since the line was coiled about various sorts of frames and no rod was used at first, the frame simply being turned so that the hand line peeled off freely. The method was never abandoned in some areas and many fishermen, still using them for a variety of fishing in both fresh and salt water, have simply substituted metal cans for the "frames."

The principle was in use in the the seventeenth century in southern Europe, and in the eighteenth century Basques were using a rod with a sort of "birdcage reel." Then came trays or body reels for holding the line. They used the spinning principle, although the device was attached to the fisherman rather than to the rod.

The Peter Malloch reel of 1884, designed in Perth, Scotland, may not have been the first true spinning reel, but it was the beginning of the course of modern development. It operated as a fixed-spool spinning reel while the cast was being made; then, when the fisherman made his retrieve, the spool was moved on a turntable so that its axis was at right angles to the cast, and the line was wound back in the manner of the conventional multiplying reel.

The disadvantage of the Malloch reel was that it twisted the line continually, and after casting for a time it was necessary for the line to be straightened in some manner. Some fishermen employed a loop splice so they could readily undo the forward section of their lines and reverse it.

The English reel of Alfred Illingworth was next. It consisted of a stationary spool with a pickup that revolved around it, thus counteracting the twist created by casting. It worked so efficiently that it was barred from many English rivers. Later developments produced improved pickup units and the bail, as well as the oscillating mechanism to spread line evenly on the spool. There were much-improved English and French reels well before spinning came to America. The Luxor reel was introduced to the United States by Bache Brown in 1935, but before the new method could gain a solid footing, war in Europe cut off the sources of equipment. When the war ended, spinning appeared as a completely new way of fishing. Some of its earliest exponents predicted that it would be the end of other methods. The rush to spinning was encouraged by the development of excellent monofilament lines.

Opening pages: "Fishing machine" boat
exemplifies modern equipment for offshore angling
and is equipped with outriggers and
twin motors. Such open boats, usually less than
23 feet long, travel at high speed
on waters once fished only by large cruisers.
Anglers shown here are landing
a large tarpon. Needles and fishhooks (below) were
kindred products of early manufacturers.

THOMAS H. BATE & CO.

No. 7 WARREN STREET,

NEW YORK,

MANUFACTURERS AND IMPORTERS OF

NEEDLES, FISH HOOKS,

FISHING RODS AND TACKLE

OF EVERY DESCRIPTION.

NEW YORK:

McCLELLAN & IVERS, STATIONERS, 66 WALL STREET.

230

American manufacturers, quickly adopting the principles of the European reels, built their own products, but imports—often under American names—continued to make up a large share of those used in the United States.

The old Malloch principle was revived in some completely enclosed American-built reels, but as there was no provision for straightening the line as it was spooled, such equipment quickly fell into disfavor. American designers, feeling they had the ultimate casting method, endeavored to make it even simpler for the user, building closed-face reels whose mechanism was hidden, except for control buttons, handles, and the emerging line. They appealed to a mechanized America and became the most widely used reels of all in fresh water. In salt water, the open-face reel remained the leader.

Spinning was efficient and the nearest thing to a method for every situation. Perhaps for this reason it was not widely banned by American law as was once expected. It settled into a special niche as the most popular method, but there still was room for other tackle, even in fresh water.

It was in casting small lures for considerable distances that the spinning outfit made its mark. Bait-casting tackle was inefficient when the lures weighed less than a quarter-ounce, and only fine casters with specialized gear could handle lures of much less than half an ounce. Small spinners and miniature plugs could be used after a fashion with fly rods, but it was not altogether satisfactory and proper retrieving was difficult. Spinning equipment was made for such tasks and game fish all over America were confronted with little lures that performed as the big bait-casting lures had always done. The results were excellent.

Trout fishermen used ultralight thread line in small brooks, throwing gleaming little spoons and spinners that could be maneuvered among the shallow rocks. Some of them attached spinning reels to their fly rods to secure the ultimate in delicate presentation.

The black-bass fishermen found they could cast small lures, hardly heavier than fly-rod bugs, and send them farther than with fly tackle. Fragile natural baits could be served with gentle tosses which did not damage them.

Some of the new spinning reels came with efficient drags, making it possible to play very large fish with very light tackle, and the spin-fishermen moved quickly to salt water, where they immediately challenged anything that would strike. Spin-fishing clubs sprang up to recognize achievements which did not quite fit other types of tackle.

A very old lure found new importance with the beginning of American spinning. The jig, the ancient weapon of commercial sea fishermen and beloved by some surf-casters, suddenly appeared as an all-around lure. Until about 1947 it was virtually unheard of in fresh-water casting, but in small sizes it was remarkably adapted to spinning in lake or ocean. The name describes its original use. It was designed to be worked up and down from a boat or through an ice hole, an action which, oddly enough, attracts fish, although such movement is uncommon in bait-fish or other game-fish quarry.

Hardly any artificial lures had been used completely against the bottom before the spinfishermen began their work, but the new masters appeared with what they called "fishing hands," a cultivated feeling for the lure's movements. The little jig is cast into fairly shallow water and retrieved slowly, so the fisherman can discern its action. It hops a few inches above the bottom, drops back to stir a tiny puff of mud or sand, and then moves forward again to hesitate once more. It is made of a lead head with a little sprig of bucktail, and it appears so helpless that the fish is in no hurry. The angler feels a gentle resistance, yet when he increases his pressure the lure comes free and he allows it to sink to the bottom again. There are other tentative tugs but the lure pulls free several times before the resistance is solid and the needle-sharp hook penetrates.

The angler has felt the fish's tentative nibbling and read its actions through his gently vibrating rod tip, and when he has tightened the line against the quarry he has not been abrupt enough to frighten it. He carries on a restrained tug of war until he is positive the fish has decided to keep his lure. Generally he knows what kind of fish he has hooked, but he is especially pleased when the tugs and runs seem unusual, for he keeps a life list of the catches he has made on his little jigs and already the species number more than a hundred, many of them fishes seldom caught with any kind of artificial.

The little jigs were shaped according to purpose and they were dressed with hair, feathers, and synthetic materials. Years after they first became popular, many of them were equipped with soft plastic tails, a logical development from the plastic worms that invaded fresh water so successfully.

The plastic worm must have begun as an imitation of the strips of pork rind that had been used for more than a hundred years by bass fishermen. It became the most successful black-bass lure ever used, gaining particular momentum during the nineteen-fifties. At first it was used almost entirely with spinning tackle. It was moved very slowly along the bottom, and the taking fish was allowed to carry it for some time before the angler struck. Then it was found that worms often were successful when reeled rapidly through water vegetation with weedless rigging. Finally, there was true surface fishing with worms that were designed to float.

Although spinning tackle continued to be preferred by most American fishermen, bait-casting tackle came on strongly again after nearly losing its following completely. There were several reasons for this, enough to insure that the turning-spool reel would have an unqualified future.

With the advent of American spinning there was a pause in the development of the turning-spool bait-casting reel. It already had acquired its important features. New alloys had made the strong, lightweight spool practical, so that the flywheel-like action of the older reels disappeared. The light spools, made for lighter lures, required less thumbing and this contributed to accuracy. The level-winding mechanism, used in various forms for generations, had become almost standard by the nineteen-thirties. Free-spooling, an arrangement whereby the handle and gears were disconnected from the spool during casting, had been used for some time on surf-casting reels and on some light tournament designs. Various antibacklash devices had been used for years to minimize the amount of thumbing necessary. Silk lines, with their attendant frailties, had been largely replaced by braided nylon, and some of the monofilament used for spinning reels also worked well on turning spools.

Some of the new lures developed for spinning were fished lightly, and when the plastic-

Three stages of lures for bass: old-time
flies (right), contemporary extremes of "impression"
baits that developed with advent
of plug-casting (below), and plastic worms, minnows,
and what-have-you which have revolutionized
bass fishing and become popular for
many other fresh- and salt-water species
on surface or at varying depths. Biologists simply
say: "They look like fish food."

worm fisherman set the hook he found he had to overcome considerable slack, a highly flexible tip, and line stretch. At this point the stiffer bait-casting rod returned. It could handle the heavy lures that were impractical for spinning. With it, of course, came the bait-casting reel—now with a free-spooling mechanism enabling it to cast lighter lures. The bait-casting outfit worked noisy surface baits better than the traditionally soft spinning rod. So the plugging rod and the spinning rod became allies rather than competitors.

Metal rods never destroyed the bamboo market, although they made inroads as early as 1900, especially for bait-casting. The modern bait-casting rod used for artificial lures had evolved from the six-foot "Chicago rod," developed from split bamboo by James M. Clark about 1885. After 1900 it largely replaced the longer Henshall bait-casting rod, and the shorter shaft was ideal for casting artificials. Popular acceptance of steel in quality rods began in 1922, when the American Fork and Hoe Company (True Temper) introduced solid metal rods employing rapier steel. In the thirties, seamless, tubular-alloy rods competed with split bamboo, but gave way to fiberglass in the fifties.

Bamboo was much frailer than metal, but when really good glues were made in the twenties one of the main objections to it vanished. Then came the Bakelite impregnation of bamboo, which made the rod almost impervious to weather and less sensitive to rough treatment. Varnishing was unnecessary with impregnation. The Orvis Company of Manchester, Vermont, provided the best-known impregnated rods, although they also have been sold by other firms. Although spinning and plugging rods were made from bamboo, it was the fly-fisherman who insisted on it, and even after highly advanced space-age materials appeared, some of the oldest names of rodmaking appeared on hand-built bamboo rods at premium prices.

Fiberglass rods appeared about the time spinning became popular. At war's end in 1945 there was a shortage of rod materials and a new demand for recreational outlets. Fiberglass filled that gap, and then nearly took over the market. Dr. Glen Havens of National City, California, who had been experimenting with fiberglass and resins since the mid-thirties, has been credited with the first tubular fiberglass rods. The Havens system employed a steel core which was extracted after the rod was finished.

Dr. Arthur Howald developed a process involving a mandrel of balsa wood, which remained inside the rod, and his system was used by the Shakespeare Company in the first widely distributed glass models. The construction used two wrappings of glass to add strength, the inner sheath with the fibers wrapped around the core, and the outer one with the fibers running longitudinally. A variation of that system continued in use after the balsa core was discontinued.

By 1949 there were several makes of fiberglass. At first there were certain characteristic actions attributed to glass, but it developed that the action depended largely on the method of construction. Nearly any bending and recoiling characteristics could be built into the rod, once the controls were understood. Fiberglass rod construction became a mathematical science, and by 1955 it was possible to produce rod action so uniform that even the expert could find no difference in the feel of individuals of a given model.

Solid fiberglass rods are more easily made than hollow ones, and less expensive. They are also heavier and more durable. After the first few years of glass use, the solid shafts were built mainly for

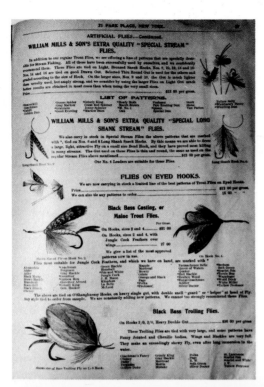

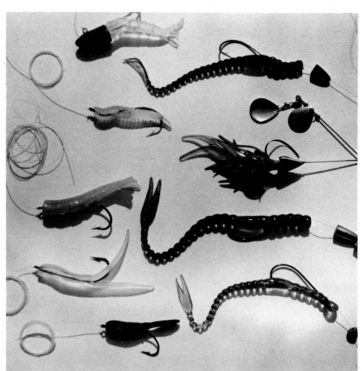

*Tarpon is one of the wildest fighters
and was the incentive for special multiplying
reels as advertised by William Mills
and Sons. Modern big-game reels are
built from salt-resistant metals
and have efficient drags to handle large, swift
offshore fish. That below
carries Dacron line. Crappie is target
of ultralight tackle of seventies.*

Current hook patterns bear same designations as those in old catalogs.

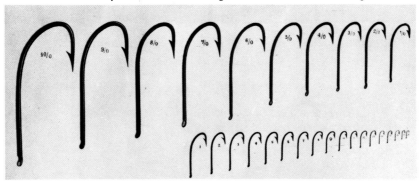

heavy-duty boat rods and for very cheap rods.

Hollow glass rods quickly reached a high level of control. By adjusting the thickness of the walls and the taper of the blank, the manufacturer could control the action meticulously. Even heavy surf sticks were made of glass, and the material was a special boon to the fly-fisherman. In bamboo the very powerful salmon fly rod was quite heavy for all-day use. When glass made powerful one-hand fly rods easy to use, it was natural for the fly-fisherman to turn to salt water, for he now had an instrument that would cast very large hair or feather streamers with a minimum of effort. He already had large-capacity fly reels for Atlantic-salmon fishing. Some of them were made even more rugged for large salt-water fish, and American builders constructed bar-stock aluminum reels with heavy-duty drags comparable to those on big-game trolling reels. The stage was set for assaults on really big fish with fly tackle, and the logical adversary was the same one that had first challenged the knuckle-buster striped-bass reels of 1885. The tarpon, of course.

Small tarpon had been caught on fly tackle when sportsmen were first discovering Florida sport fishing. Before 1912, A. W. Dimock and others had told of playing large ones on a fly rod from a canoe on Florida's west coast. Dimock's *Book of the Tarpon* showed spectacular photographs of leaping fish hooked both on fly and bait. Sometimes the canoe would be overturned during landing operations.

But with tough glass rods and reels that could withstand the expansion of great lengths of line, and with more knowledge of the fish's habits, anglers of the Florida Keys began what amounted to a new sport after World War II. They sought record tarpon on the fly, and when hundred-pound catches be-

came fairly commonplace, the fly rod was used on offshore billfish and other game heretofore considered catchable only by trollers and bait fishermen.

THE TARPON AGAIN

The fishermen are specialists and their tackle has been prepared with care. The rod has been chosen more for toughness than for its casting qualities, but it can throw the six-inch streamer far enough in expert hands. The big reel carries Dacron backing, selected because it stretches very little, and the short leader contains a foot-long section of 15-pound monofilament to meet contest requirements. There is a very heavy 80-pound tippet to meet the abrasion of a big fish's mouth, and the leader splices are carefully studied knots invented for the purpose.

The outboard boat is made for the task, swift and shallow draft, and one of the fishermen can pole it backward from the bow, using a fiberglass pushpole with a wooden foot which he sets carefully against the bottom to avoid noise.

But today's plan is for ambush rather than stalking, and the boat is anchored in three feet of clear Keys water at the edge of a deeper channel where the bottom is hardly visible. The anchor lies in plain sight on a carpet of turtle grass and is attached to a buoy, so it can be abandoned in an emergency and found later.

The tide is running out and the fishermen know that tarpon will move downstream through the channel, coming from feeding grounds which, as the tide lowers, will soon be too shallow. Already a great blue heron has alighted on a feeding station that was too deeply submerged only a short while ago. The boat is at the outer rim of a chain of flats along the Keys, only half a mile offshore, and traffic is visible on one long bridge. The islands are a low silhouette stretching to the southwest, but their distant pattern is marked by a chain of clouds which hang low above them and leave the nearby flats in bright sunshine.

Along the little channel the movement is toward deep water. A school of mullet passes in a fidgety but close-knit formation. Small barracuda seem less anxious to follow the falling tide, but several sharks glide along the channel. A hundred yards from the channel's edge, where the water has become really shallow, a bonefish's tail glistens momentarily and there are flicks of water where something tiny has fled from the bonefish's investigations.

The tarpon are first sighted a long way off. One of them makes a heavy splash striking at something and from then on the fishermen can follow the group's progress along the edge of the channel. They roll at intervals, their fins appearing briefly, and the sun occasionally flashes on their scales.

One of the fishermen is ready to cast, his heavy line coiled on the deck at his feet, his orange streamer held in the fingers of one hand while the other holds the rod. As the pod of half a dozen tarpon nears the boat their progress is noted for a time only by a little surface disturbances. Then one of them rolls to show his long back and the school becomes visible under water, a shifting patch of uncertain light and shadow in shimmering, greenish water. The fisherman's polarized glasses cut much of the glare and he selects his fish, a six-foot shadow a little nearer than the others.

There will be only one or two chances, for the fish are moving briskly. The caster waits until his target is within sixty feet and casts at right angles to its course, the big streamer some distance ahead of the fish. He retrieves it swiftly in regular foot-long pulls, so that it crosses just ahead of the tarpon's nose. The fish turns slightly to take the fly, then makes a more abrupt turn with it, churning the water but still in no hurry. When he sees his fly has disappeared, the fisherman waits until he feels a pull as the fish turns away, possibly having seen the boat, and then he sets the hook. The fish makes a short run with a boiling wake and goes high in the air; the fisherman can see a speck of color where his streamer is lodged in one corner of the gaping mouth.

It takes less than half an hour to bring the fish alongside, even though it weighs one hundred pounds, for the tarpon angler and his equipment have come a long way from the day when it was said no man would ever be able to catch a large tarpon on rod and reel.

When the fish jumps, the angler pushes his rod straight at it to give slack and prevent a break-off. When the tarpon is back in the water, he increases pressure instantly. After a few runs he finds he is able to turn his fish against the reel's drag. Before long the fish is working within fifty feet of the boat, which has been unsnapped from its anchor and has followed the tarpon along the channel.

In several feet of water the angler works firmly against a tired and discouraged fish, and when it attempts to begin a new effort he pushes his slender rod tip toward the bottom and the fish actually pauses in its beginning run and turns head down, its tail coming out as it describes a slow underwater somersault. Then, with both hands on the fly rod, the fisherman continues his pressure until the tarpon is beside the boat on its side. It is not a record fish, and his friend

*Northern pike fights angler in
outboard canoe. Ice fishing for pickerel by
19th-century anglers borrowed from
Indian methods, but was aided by skates and
tip-ups. Float plane (opposite)
carries inflatable boat to wilderness waters,
is sometimes used for fish spotting.
Simplified reels have made fishing possible
for crowds using spinning tackle.*

gaffs it gently through a lip so it can be released. They look about for their anchor buoy. The tide is well out now and if they wish to do more fishing they will have to find a new spot. The fly rod has accomplished what was once considered a task for a harpoon.

NEW SCHOOLS

The materials and skills that vanquished giant fish for record seekers made fishing more pleasant for those who dealt only in panfish.

The bluegill angler had long been a user of fly tackle, but with the availability of ultralight spinning gear he found a new approach for those days when flies were not producing well. His efforts were largely unsung, and sunfish are seldom news, but he developed tiny lures and delicate rods that were to be found in a thousand sporting goods stores near fresh-water lakes and rivers.

Very light spinning lures required small-diameter lines, and nylon monofilament was finally developed to the point that it could be made hard or soft, limp or stiff, and hairlike in size. The ultralight spinfisherman went as far as 2-pound test and there were tiny reels to match. His lures were then reduced to fit his tackle.

The tiny spoons and spinners that served for trout also worked on the small bluegills, pumpkinseeds, green sunfish, yellow perch, rock bass, and their relatives, and although there were no breathtaking leaps or smashing strikes the skill required made the game worthwhile. Near the cities, where bass and trout had disappeared, there were panfish to be magnified by delicate equipment.

The pickerel held forth in weed-choked lakes over much of the nation, and light spin-ning gear made it a true game fish, a slim assassin in miniature that rushed fiercely at quickly reeled little spinners, spoons, and pork strips.

Light spinning tackle and the new fly equipment were quick to challenge the northern pike, and even the muskellunge, and if the larger specimens were too much the fisherman soon found a fish to fit his gear.

The white bass of the great impoundments were the right size for spinning gear, and their frothy attacks on schooling menhaden brought specialists who used lures to match the bait in many cases. The "schooling" black bass of southern rivers and lakes also were ideal targets for spinning equipment; it used to take a long while to achieve "school bass" accuracy with plugging tackle.

In the lakes, groups of bass were suspended over deep water much of the time, often under shimmering schools of bait-fish, and their rushes sometimes brought them clear of the surface as they broke the shoals of bait into frantic disorganization. Such "jump bass" followed the bait during their feeding periods and only mobile fishermen could keep them in sight. The anglers hurried to the area of striking, stopped their motors, and cast before the fish "went down." The technique became a science for the black basses and the white bass. The white bass, scorned for its small size until light tackle and large impoundments arrived, became an increasingly popular game fish in the twentieth century, and its range was widened over most of the United States. Before its popularity increased it was found only south of the Great Lakes and between the Alleghenies and the Mississippi.

Spinning equipment and fast-turning bait-casting reels that worked well with light lures produced a cult of school-bass fishermen on a few southern rivers, anglers who waited for the fish to "come up" at known "schooling grounds." These were generally created by a bottom formation which caused schools of traveling bait to become confused, or compressed them over a bar where there was a current.

School-bass experts learned the locations of striking grounds, some of which were the same for generations, and visited them regularly when bait was running in the river. The boat was anchored within convenient casting distance of where the fish were expected to come up, and when the first bait skipped the good caster tried to drop his lure between the bait and its pursuer. Such "rallies" of feeding fish were sometimes very brief, with opportunity for only a single hurried cast, and it became a specialized sport.

When school-bass fishing was at its peak the plastic worm became popular, and some fishermen learned to fish it on the bottom beneath the schooling spots, hoping to catch the fish after they had retired to wait for a new school of bait. Spinning tackle probably caught more schooling bass than any other method, but it was not responsible for the gradual fading of the sport. Bass populations declined in most streams through the pressures of civilization. Only fifteen years after school fishing reached its peak on the rivers, there are few school-bass fishermen practicing their sport and the old information grapevines do not exist. Some of the veterans say the "jump" bass have changed their ways and others say they are gone from the rivers. They still appear on the lakes.

CROWDS OF FISHERMEN

Population growth was not the only reason for increasing numbers of fishermen after 1950. Pleasure boating

Winslow Homer's "Pike, Lake St. John."

became a leading pastime and outboard motors reached new levels of power and reliability. Americans showed special interest in travel trailers and live-aboard vehicles, as well as in larger boats suitable for overnight trips for fish and game. The fisherman wanted to see what was around the bend.

Even before the bass boat appeared in the Midwest and South, there was something new in boating, a craft soon to be called the "fishing machine." It was generally outboard powered, it was fast, it was wide open for fishing, it was capable of operating in the open sea or on very large lakes, it had electronic depthfinding and navigation equipment, it could be trailered—and it was much less expensive than the larger sportfisherman. The small fishing machine is not inexpensive, but it is within the reach of anglers who cannot afford a fully equipped offshore cruiser. It is a part of an enormous boating industry that seems to survive and grow regardless of business conditions or competition from other recreation.

Those who build fishing tackle, boats, and the other things used by anglers have sought to make fishing the most democratic of sports and have

*Latest fly-fishing tackle, shown
with brown trout, features graphite rod and
ultralight fly reel in contrast
to bulky equipment of 100 years before. Waders
were seldom used until recent years.
Canoe (opposite) is not only romantic craft for
use on wilderness waters, but has
proved highly effective for modern fishing and
is now made of space-age materials.*

succeeded remarkably. Although there is place for the highly skilled expert who casts tiny flies for sophisticated trout, or the competitor who plays sailfish on 6-pound monofilament line, there are millions who fish in the simplest manner for the fish easiest to catch. The tackle, resort, and guiding industries and the managers of fish populations have considered them. As in other recreation, there is some difference in the requirements of the casual participant and the expert.

Controlled situations are necessary for the simplest fishing, even as the tackle requires no great·experience. On some large impoundments there are floating fishing docks, heated for winter fishing, where large numbers of crappie fishermen can enjoy comfortable chairs, carpets, television, and restaurants without going ashore. The crappie barge or dock was an established institution in the early thirties, but in the fifties it was refined and is used by thousands. Although crappie are the most common catch, such fishing also produces white bass, catfish, and largemouth bass. The fishing dock is most popular in winter. Submerged trees are used to provide special attraction, along with bags of chum and appropriate lighting for night fishing.

Ice fishing has been refined by the use of gleaming modern descendants of the "dark hut" of primitive Americans; the term "ice shanty" is hardly appropriate for the comfortable fishing cottages towed on runners by tractors or snow machines on northern lakes. The ice is used as a convenient conveyor of "artificial reefs" on some fresh water, fishermen placing heaps of weighted brush on the ice to await

spring thaw. The sunken obstacles attract a variety of panfish, as well as bass or pike.

On all coasts the party boat is ready for those willing to fish in the company of others. It takes passengers long distances at low cost, usually for bottom-fishing, with bait and tackle furnished. Such craft are usually equipped with the most advanced electronic equipment, and the beginner is aided by mates skilled in the game.

The traveling fisherman is recognized by concerns ready to deliver package tours for any part of the world, and especially northern Canada and Latin America, a result of swift air transportation and the crowding of waters nearer to the angler's home. It is possible for an angler to take a carefully planned trip that will produce the subtropical bonefish and the Arctic char within the same twenty-four hours. If there is no such thing as virgin fishing water today, there is at least wilderness water, where fishermen are few and far between.

THE FISHERMAN FLIES

The float plane has been the fisherman's key to isolated waters of the Far North, a device that deposits him on timbered and mountain-rimmed lakes in a transition so sudden that he feels out of place and still imagines he hears the roar of traffic in the distance. But at first he really hears only the fading sound of the plane that brought him as it disappears over the treetops and the scuffling noises of his companion stowing their equipment in the rough cabin. He does not even notice the loon's cry until his ears have tuned to the wilderness, as they have done on earlier trips. He sees the widening circles of a fish's movement near the shore, where a fallen cedar has lain for years, its partly rotted top submerged in clear, chilly water.

It is late evening, but this far north there will be little darkness in summer. It is a long way to any road. The maps show them as very thin lines in that part of British Columbia, like the small tributary streams of a main river, but there are none near the little lake, and as he moves into the cabin he wonders at the amount of work it has required to transport its Spartan furnishings by air.

The canoe is light and small, having arrived as an air passenger itself, and when the two fishermen slide away from shore with it they do so smoothly as befits old friends who have used canoes together before. They paddle silently and watch the loon fly to another part of the little lake, and they are in no hurry to use their rods.

The tackle is good but simple, sturdy bait-casting rods with heavy monofilament line, and a short wire leader with a large red and white spoon. The spoon sails accurately toward the end of the old fallen cedar and strikes the water with a splat. It sinks briefly, making an erratic series of flashes as it goes down, and then starts back toward the canoe in a swinging, searching movement. The pike does not wait long but catches it in his teeth, as if he intends to shake it, and when he is hooked he jumps once and then comes up to thrash the water with his head, his mouth wide open. Two smaller fish follow him, one of them trying to take the spoon for himself, and even when the hooked fish is brought to the canoe and gingerly released the pursuers are reluctant to leave.

On another cast a fish strikes and is not hooked, and when the fisherman sees it following at rod's length, its angry eyes on the lure, he submerges his rod tip, swinging the spoon back and forth under water, and the fish attacks swiftly. The fishing is almost too easy, but the fishermen have known it would be so. Although they have caught very difficult fish with great effort in other places, they have come back to the wilderness for the loon's call and the howl of the wolf they hope they may hear at night. They would feel farther away from the city if they had come laboriously on horseback or with backpacks, but there is not that much time, and on the appointed day they watch for the speck of seaplane that will drop to their little lake and take them back. By then they have begun to feel at home and no longer like intruders.

AN END PRODUCT

The rod weighs less than two ounces and is made of graphite. William Watt of England first utilized the material in 1965 and it had been used extensively in aerospace before being adapted to rod building. By 1975 it was proving popular, although more expensive than glass. It had proved to be very light and strong, and it seemed certain that rod action could be adapted to the needs of a variety of fishermen, probably actions that could compete with split bamboo, as fiberglass had already done.

The reel is a lightweight alloy and so skeletonized that it matches the rod's balance. The line is high-floating and accurately tapered by a machine which shapes it to an exact weight. The fisherman uses a fly that will float high because of a silicone preparation that has been applied, and the carefully tapered leader carries a tippet that is hair-thin but tests almost two pounds.

The stream flows under a bridge of stone and logs, widens a little, and then is pinched again by a carefully designed structure that causes the current to dig a pocket below it. In the pocket are several trout, now rising occasionally to take small insects. There is a bench a little back from the brook's shore and one fisherman sits there to wait for a better rise. The path along the creek is well used, both by fishermen and by dairy cattle that stroll along and occasionally roil the stream by wading in the shallow parts.

At one side of the brook is a series of trout-rearing ponds and a pump there makes a considerable noise. There are stiles along the fence between the ponds and the creek, and there are several cars in a small parking lot.

The fisherman in the water watches the trout rising below the small diversion dam and decides his fly matches the hatch satisfactorily. He moves to one side a little so that he can get a proper drift across the feeding area and begins to work out line with his tiny rod.

The trout were raised in the pools across the fence, but they have been in the creek for some time and the less perceptive of them have already been caught. The fisherman knows he will have to make a good presentation, but he would not have joined the club if the fishing had been too easy, for membership is very expensive.

There are kinds of fishing, especially those for the polished master, which have become difficult to find and often expensive. Wilderness fishing has become less plentiful for the very reasons that have made it quickly available. As he dammed free-flowing rivers, man built his own easily reached fishing waters for the multitude. And although America's fish face increasing thousands of fishermen, they have acquired as many allies in the continuing fight to preserve their ranges.

Bibliography

Babson, Stanley M., *Bonefishing*. New York, Winchester, rev. ed., 1973.

Bethune, George Washington, ed., *The Compleat Angler*. American edition, 1847.

Brooks, Joe, *Trout Fishing*. New York, Harper & Row, 1972.

Brown, John J., *American Angler's Guide*. New York, Appleton, 1876.

Chase, Mary Ellen, *The Fishing Fleets of New England*. Boston, Houghton Mifflin, 1961.

Dimock, A. W., *Book of the Tarpon*. London, 1912.

Drucker, Philip, *Indians of the Northwest Coast*. Garden City, NY, Natural History, 1963.

Forester, Frank (Henry William Herbert), *The Complete Manual for Young Sportsmen*. New York, George E. Woodward, 1856.

Gabrielson, Ira N., and LaMonte, Francesca, *The New Fisherman's Encyclopedia*. Harrisburg, PA, Stackpole, 1950.

Gemming, Elizabeth, *Blow Ye Winds Westerly*. New York, Crowell, 1971.

Gifford, Tommy, *Anglers and Muscleheads*. New York, Dutton, 1960.

Gingrich, Arnold, *The Fishing in Print*. New York, Winchester, 1974.

Gresham, Grits, *Complete Book of Bass Fishing*. New York, Outdoor Life, Harper & Row, 1966.

Grey, Zane, *Tales of Fishes*. New York, Harper, 1919.

Halford, Frederic, *Floating Flies and How to Dress Them*. 1886.

Henshall, Dr. James A., *Bass, Pike, Perch & Other Game Fishes of North America*, Cincinnati, 1919.

—————— *Book of the Black Bass*, Cincinnati, Clarke, 1904.

Hewitt, E. R., *A Trout and Salmon Fisherman for Seventy-five Years*. New York, Abercrombie & Fitch, Ann Arbor University Microfilms, 1966.

Holcomb, Dennis, *Introduction of Fishes to Michigan Waters*. School of Natural Resources, University of Michigan, 1964.

Holder, Charles Frederick, *The Log of A Sea Angler*. Boston, Houghton Mifflin, 1906.

Karas, Nicholas, *The Complete Book of the Striped Bass*. New York, Winchester, 1974.

Koller, Larry, *The Treasury of Angling*. New York, Ridge/Golden, 1963.

LaFarge, Oliver, *A Pictorial History of the American Indian*. New York, Crown, 1956.

Lyman, Henry, *Bluefishing*. New York, Barnes, 1955.

—————— *The Complete Book of Weakfishing*. New York, Barnes, 1959.

—————— and Woolner, Frank, *The Complete Book of Striped Bass Fishing*. New York, Barnes, 1954.

McClane, A. J., *McClane's Standard Fishing Encyclopedia*. New York, Holt, Rinehart and Winston, 1974.

McDonald, John, *Quill Gordon*. New York, Knopf, 1972.

Melner, Samuel, and Kessler, Hermann, *Great Fishing Tackle Catalogs of the Golden Age*. New York, Crown, 1972.

Migdalski, Edward C., *Angler's Guide to the Fresh Water Sport Fishes of North America*. New York, Ronald, 1962.

Miles, Charles, *Indian and Eskimo Artifacts of North America*. Chicago, Regnery, 1963.

Moser, Commander Jefferson F., *Alaska Salmon and Salmon Fisheries*. Washington, DC, Government Printing Office, 1899.

Moss, Frank T., *Successful Striped Bass Fishing*. Camden, ME, International Marine, 1974.

Needham, Paul, *Trout Streams*. New York, Winchester, 1969.

Netboy, Anthony, *The Atlantic Salmon, A Vanishing Species?* London, Faber and Faber, 1968.

—————— *Salmon of the Pacific Northwest*. Portland, OR, Metropolitan, 1958.

Norris, Thaddeus, *The American Angler's Book*. Philadelphia, Porter and Coates, 1864.

Reiger, George, *Profiles in Salt Water Angling*. Englewood Cliffs, NJ, Prentice-Hall, 1973.

Reinfelder, Al, *Bait Tail Fishing*. New York, Barnes, 1969.

Roosevelt, Robert B., *Superior Fishing*. New York, Carleton, 1865.

St. John, Larry, *Practical Bait Casting*. New York, Macmillan, 1920.

Salter, T. F., *The Angler's Guide*. London, Carpenter, 1823.

Scott, Genio C., *Fishing In American Waters*. New York, Harper, 1869.

Skues, G. E. M., *Nymph Fishing for Chalk Stream Trout*. London, 1939.

Sosin, Mark, and Clark, John, *Through the Fish's Eye*. New York, Harper & Row, 1973.

Trench, Charles Chenevix, *A History of Angling*. Chicago, Follett, 1974.

United States Department of the Interior, *Sport Fishing U.S.A*. Bureau of Sports Fishing and Wildlife, Washington, D.C.

Walker, C. F., *The Art of Chalk Stream Fishing*. Harrisburg, PA, Stackpole, 1968.

Woolner, Frank, *Modern Saltwater Sport Fishing*. New York, Crown, 1972.

Wulff, Lee, *The Atlantic Salmon*. New York, Barnes, 1958.

Picture Credits

CHAPTER 1

10-11: EAB. 15: Bruce Coleman; Henry and Vera Bradshaw; Jane
Burton, BC. 17: Rare Book Division, NYPL. 18: Nicholas deVore III,
BC. 19: WS; EAB; Steve McCutcheon. 21: Royal Ontario Museum,
Toronto. 22: EAB. 24: Stark Museum of Art, Orange, Texas. 25: Public
Archives of Canada. 26: Stark Museum of Art. 27: CW.

CHAPTER 2

30-31: NYPL. 34-35: GC. 35 & 36: The Bettmann Archive.
37: NYPL. 38: R. Thompson, BC. 40 & 41: CP. 42: EAB; Doug Wilson;
L. M. Stone, BC. 43: Doug Wilson. 46: EAB. 47: CFW; EAB.

CHAPTER 3

50-51: Abby Aldrich Rockefeller Folk Art Collection, Williamsburg,
Virginia. 55: Guildhall Library, London; Yale University Library;
Yale University Library. 56: Rare Book Division, NYPL; 57: NYPL.
59: EAB. 61: Butler Institute of American Art, Youngstown, Ohio.
62: WC; Library of Congress. 63: Smithsonian Institution,
Harry T. Peters "America on Stone" Lithography Collection. 64: NYPL.
65: Yale University Library. 66-67: The Harry T. Peters Collection,
Museum of the City of New York. 68: Library of Congress.

CHAPTER 4

70-71: WS. 74: IBM Corporation. 75: WS; WC;
Museum of Fine Arts, Boston, M & M Karolik Collection. 76 & 78: NYPL.
79: Private Collection, photograph Davis & Long Co. 80: CP.
82: WS. 83, 85 & 86: NYPL. 86-87: Berry-Hill Galleries, Inc. 89: The
Museums at Stony Brook, Stony Brook, L.I., Melville
Collection; Harry T. Peters "America on Stone" Lithography
Collection, Smithsonian Institution. 90: WS.

CHAPTER 5

94-95: CFW. 98: Courtesy of Roy Steenrod and
Outdoor Life; CP. 99: WS. 101: Harry T. Peters "America on Stone"
Lithography Collection, Smithsonian Institution. 102:
James Tallon; WC; WC; EAB. 103: WC, photograph Albert Squillace.
104: Metropolitan Museum of Art, from the collection of Miss A. S.
Colgate. 105: NYPL. 106: WS. 107: WC; CP. 108: Library of Congress.
110: WC. 111: Library of Congress; CFW. 112: NYPL.
115: The Butler Institute of American Art, Youngstown, Ohio.

CHAPTER 6

118-119: CFW. 121: NYPL. 122: James Tallon. 123: EAB;
Russell Tinsley; Oliver B. James Collection of American Art,
Arizona State University. 124: Library of Congress. 126-127: EAB.
128: NYPL. 131: CFW; Leonard Lee Rue III; Henry and
Vera Bradshaw; James Tallon; Oxford Scientific Films, BC.
134: Tom Wendelburg. 135: CFW; Tom Wendelburg.
136: EAB. 137: Doug Wilson. 139: Burton McNeely; CFW.

CHAPTER 7

142-143: Bob Gelberg. 145: GC. 146: EAB. 148: NYPL.
150-151: Jen and Des Bartlett, BC. 150: Burton McNeely. 151: Jen
and Des Bartlett, BC. 153: EAB. 154-155: CFW.
155: Norman M. Strung; Russell Tinsley. 156-157: Doug Wilson;
all others, James Tallon. 158: Mark J. Sosin. 160: EAB.
160-161: Doug Wilson. 163: EAB. 164: Doug Wilson. 165 & 167: EAB.

CHAPTER 8

170-171: Mark J. Sosin. 174-175: The Bettmann Archive.
175 & 176: NYPL. 178: James Tallon. 181: EAB. 182: CFW. 183: EAB.
184-185: bottom left, Mark J. Sosin; all others CFW.
186: Burton McNeely; GC. 187: EAB. 188: Harry T. Peters "America
on Stone" Lithography Collection, Smithsonian Institution. 189: EAB.
190-191: GC; EAB. 193: American Philosophical Society Library.

CHAPTER 9

194-195: Frank Eck. 197: UPI. 198: Steve McCutcheon. 199: Josephus
Daniels, Rapho-Guillumette. 201: GC. 202: Novosti from Sovfoto;
Tass from Sovfoto. 203: Novosti from Sovfoto; Novosti from Sovfoto;
Tass from Sovfoto. 205: NYPL. 206: UPI. 208: NYPL. 209: CFW; CFW;
NYPL. 210: CFW. 211: Paul D. McLain. 212-213: EAB. 214: CFW.
214-215: CP. 218-219: CFW. 221: Museum of Fine Arts, Boston. 223:
Burton McNeely. 225: Georgia Museum of Art Collection.

CHAPTER 10

226-227: Burton McNeely. 229: WC. 233: WC; EAB; EAB.
234: EAB. 235: WC; CFW; CFW. 236: WC. 238: EAB; NYPL.
239: EAB; Doug Wilson. 241: Fogg Art Museum, Cambridge, Mass.
242: CFW; NYPL. 243: Norman M. Strung. 252: The Harry T. Peters
Collection, Museum of the City of New York.

Pastoral scene of successful sport
would please either Izaak Walton or a
modern fisherman. Currier & Ives
have related hunting and fishing in "Good Luck
All Around." Shorebirds and grouse
fill hunter's bag and fisherman's creel overflows
with large trout. Angler playing fish
in background has a ready assistant standing
by with long-handled net.